IN PRAISE OF

"**Discover Your Hidden Self** *is a delightful book – easy to read, but thought provoking and life changing if put into practice. The book is a well-balanced mix of stories and calls to action. John Murray pulls no punches. He readily admits life is often difficult and circumstances unfair, but he reminds us of the power of reflection, meditation, forgiveness, reaching out to others, having a positive attitude, and faith in God. I highly recommend you read this book and share it with others you know who are struggling with challenges in their lives."*

Ruth L. Snyder, Author, Creativity & Book Coach.
Past President of Inscribe Christian Writers' Fellowship.

"With a remarkable ability to observe and interpret the human experience, John Murray challenges you to look deep within yourself — to understand who you are in light of the life you have lived. He invites you to consider how your experiences have formed you, encouraging clear thinking and a positive attitude, despite the rough times you may face.

Discover Your Hidden Self *is a conversation with a friend who encourages you to recognize your potential, to seize the positive side of life, to step outside yourself and serve others, and to be content with being your ordinary self. And without intruding or imposing, the author gently prods you toward the God who created you, loves you, and invites you to build your life in relationship with him."*

David Daniels, Fellowship Baptist Pastor (Retired)
Freelance Book Reviewer.

"Hardship, misfortune and misery are universal among us but explanations and solutions are not. With intimate empathy born from personal experience, John Murray brings remedy. In twelve short chapters Murray astutely covers a wide world of our human frailties, trauma, anxieties and fears. This is practical multi-dimensional help, referencing verifiable life stories, expert professional opinions and faith-based guidance. **Discover Your Hidden Self** reads effortlessly, yet chapter by chapter the content invites honesty, self-examination, ownership, self-help, and reliance on God. In the process of encouraging a reader's mental, emotional and spiritual health, this author enables readers to have compassion and to be an encouragement and an agent for change in others."

Dr. Ron Unruh, Author, Artist and Advocate.
Past President of the Evangelical Free Churches of Canada.

"I enjoyed and was impressed in reading **Discover Your Hidden Self**. It is an extremely well written book. John Murray describes life in an interesting, convincing, simplified and understandable way. Its message comes through clearly as a lesson for living. I believe the book will be effective in providing inspiration and encouragement to its readers. It has my full recommendation."

Bill Vander Zalm, Former Mayor of Surrey, B.C., and Former Premier of the Province of British Columbia, Canada.

"John Murray writes from a wealth of personal experience. He has lived through many difficult circumstances and has demonstrated an unusual ability to deal with situations that would embitter many. He has a profound sense of the reality of God's love. The book shows that John Murray knows whereof he writes"

David North, B.Ed., M.Ed. Retired Principal, Lions Gate Christian Academy.

"John Murray is a thoughtful, engaging writer. In his book **Discover Your Hidden Self***, he is relentlessly positive and encouraging. John is a true Barnabas, a son of encouragement. This book tells many engaging true stories of people who faced impossible odds, yet found a way forward. I was impressed to read of John, "having reached (his) ninth decade and closing in on sixty years of marriage." His literary perseverance and hopefulness is an inspiration to others. As John says, 'We don't have to be prisoners of our circumstances. Be encouraged because there is hope.' John's book can be summed up in his own words: 'Remember, you are your own person. You are unique. You are special. You are exceptional.' Thank God for such a positive person in this fearful age."*

Rev. Dr. Ed Hird. Author and Conference Speaker.

"John Murray has written a wonderful book in **Discover Your Hidden Self**. *It emphasizes the importance of living mindfully. He asks an important question 'Are you contented?' which calls for an answer but maybe calls for us to face a change. Perhaps, however, by changing ourselves, we can change the world for the better!"*

John O'Brien, M.D.

"The older you get the more suffering you will inevitably experience. If you want a guide to help you navigate the significant challenges life will send your way, don't look for someone young. John Murray has walked through some difficult decades. He has learned not only from his own experience but from many others. Their stories and lessons are found throughout the book. Our author has found comfort from God in his own troubles, as you can be comforted and taught in yours."

Dr. Adrian Warnock, Psychiatrist, Author of *Hope Reborn*.

DISCOVER YOUR HIDDEN SELF

OPENING THE DOOR TO WHO YOU REALLY ARE

John Murray

DISCOVER YOUR HIDDEN SELF
Opening the Door to Who You Really Are

Copyright © John Murray, 2020

All rights reserved. No part of this publication may be reproduced, stored in a retrieval system, or transmitted in any form or by any means, electronic, mechanical, photocopying, recording, or otherwise, without written permission of the author and publisher.

Published by John Murray, White Rock, Canada

Cover design and photography: Roger E. Murray

ISBN 0-978-1-77354-221-8

Publication assistance and digital printing in Canada by

PageMaster.ca

Contents

INTRODUCTION: How Deep Is Your River?............... 1

CHAPTER 1: Living in the Shadow 5

CHAPTER 2: When Life Seems Unfair 13

CHAPTER 3: Order out of Chaos 23

CHAPTER 4: Our Thinking Is Critical 33

CHAPTER 5: Our Attitude Says It All 45

CHAPTER 6: Forgiveness Is a Tough Call 57

CHAPTER 7: Why Do We Crave Significance? 69

CHAPTER 8: It's Okay to be Ordinary 79

CHAPTER 9: Touch a Person – Change a Life........... 91

CHAPTER 10: Who Is My Neighbour? 103

CHAPTER 11: Life Is a Spiritual Encounter 111

CHAPTER 12: The Real You 121

NOTES 126

ABOUT THE AUTHOR... 132

INTRODUCTION

How Deep Is Your River?

Our lives are like rivers. At times the water runs deep, smooth and quiet. It glides by peacefully, silently, without a ripple. At other times it is shallow and the water explodes, gurgles, and splashes over the rocks, struggling to find the easiest path as it rushes downstream. Life is like that. We experience comfortable times when we feel satisfied and contented. Everything seems to fit together and run smoothly. Then come the times when things are anything but smooth. What can go wrong seems to go wrong. The rocks and obstacles are hard and they hurt. It's at those times that we call upon our inner physical, mental, and spiritual resources to help us. So, how deep is your river? Is it running smoothly or is it turbulent right now?

None of us can avoid the tough times. Even as I write, the world is struggling with the devastating effects of the coronavirus pandemic, an event which has caused suffering in every corner of the globe. From the millions of people who contracted the virus, hundreds of thousands have succumbed to its deadly touch. Families have had their lives shattered as they have lost loved ones to an unexpected and early death. The pandemic has changed the shape of our society but with it has changed our personal living environments and brought untold pain.

The pandemic aside, occasionally events sideswipe us. Accidents happen, and tragically our lives can change overnight. Unexpectedly, we are faced with hard issues. We lose our job. Our spouse or child suddenly becomes seriously ill. We suffer severed relationships through misunderstandings. We discover our child is being bullied at school. A financial bombshell hits us. Stress builds daily, and on it goes. I am sure you can add to the list.

Our lives often become a litany of crises. We begin to fear what might be around the corner. Consequently, for some, life hurts and becomes hard to handle. No quick ready-made formula appears on the scene to change the situation. We become physically spent, mentally exhausted, and spiritually stretched. Some may even wonder, "Is this really what God intended for me?"

Having reached my ninth decade, and closing in on sixty years of marriage, I can testify that we cannot possibly avoid all of life's obstacles. Life is no respecter of persons in handing out illnesses and accidents. However, my wife and I have found that, although the hard knocks of life bring you low, tenacity and faith can lift you up. We were ill-prepared for some things thrown at us, but we discovered that there is always sunshine after the storm, always light after the darkness, always peace after the turmoil. How grateful we have been to experience a silver lining in the dark clouds. Hence, I write and share with you out of that experience.

In this book, I readily admit that we humans have to face struggles and battles daily, but we look for solutions. These are not always simple or easy to find. If you are struggling at this moment with emotional or inter-personal relationship problems, be assured there is a solution. It may already be within you or it may have to come from an outside source. Either way, finding the solution—getting yourself on an even keel, and finding strength to face life's issues—is the primary objective. The resolution may be natural and physical, or it could even be spiritual, something we often overlook in our humanness. We need a balance. We need to check out both the natural and spiritual aspects of our lives.

Being human, we become anxious and stressed. We get angry at life and ask questions like, "Why?" Why me? Why us? Why now? And that's good. Because until we ask questions, we get no answers. Hopefully, this book will help you find answers and a fresh perspective on your life.

Do you want to be encouraged? Do you want to be rid of emotional turmoil and move into a place of calmness and serenity? Are you looking for confidence and control in your life? Then read on. Be prepared to see yourself reflected in the following pages. If you do, you will find yourself in good company. You will find that others have been down your path and have bounced back. They found a solution, a way out. If life can change for others, why not for you?

CHAPTER 1

Living in the Shadow

We live in the shadow of yesterday's choices. We live with the consequences of yesterday's mistakes. Many of us live with regrets. Some of us are haunted by seemingly wasted years. We live with the frustration that we cannot turn the clock back. If we knew some time ago what we know now, perhaps we would have made different choices.

Is your life a struggle? Have you been hurt? Have you become disillusioned with life? Are you down on yourself? This is not how your life needs to be. I want to help you turn your back on the ghosts of yesterday and walk into a new life, one lived in the light of a new awareness, with new decisions and new choices. Choices that bring help, healing, and enjoyment. Whatever problems yesterday brought you, I want tomorrow to be different for you.

The adversity of life hits all of us in different ways and at various times. For some it hit very early being born with a physical disability. For others it came later through accident, illness, or abuse. Regardless of origin, how it happened, or when it happened, how we respond to it is the secret to coming out on top. In the pages ahead we will share stories of people who refused to let those adversities put them on the sidelines. Stories of people who exercised determination to rise above their circumstances.

Take the story of Nicholas McCarthy. Nicholas was born without a right hand. In 2012, he graduated as a pianist from the Royal College of Music in London, England. In the college's 130-year history, he was the first student with one hand to graduate. At fourteen, Nicholas told his mother he wanted to be a concert pianist. Whether or not his mother laughed at the idea I don't know, but she must have had some negative thoughts pass through her mind, such as, "How do you expect to do that with one hand?" Nicholas would not be deterred. He tried to teach himself to play, and then had two years of professional teaching.

He tried hard to get into a music school, only to be refused more than once because of his disability. Exercising some perseverance, he applied to a school of dance and music. He did not reveal his handicap until he showed up at the audition. His competence at the piano earned him a place at the school, but he wasn't finished yet. His heart was set on the Royal College of Music. Amazingly, he again managed to get the door open, and boldly he went through it. To his delight, in his research he discovered music written for one-handed players. He worked hard, graduated, and a few months after graduation was playing in front of 86,000 people at the closing ceremony of the Para-Olympics in London.

Since then, McCarthy has travelled the world as a concert pianist. He achieved his goal by sheer determination and sticking to his plan. At any point, he could have given up, especially in the early days, and no one would have thought badly of him, but that was not in his mind or in his nature. He could have sat at home and bemoaned his lot, but he chose not to do that. How different life might have been had he succumbed to the expected limitation of being one-handed. He refused to allow his disadvantage to win.

In the end McCarthy probably achieved more than he had even imagined. He discovered that very little is handed to you. You have to go after it, chase it down, and pursue the dream to the end.

SUFFERING IS UNIVERSAL

Jordan Peterson says in his book *12 Rules for Life,* "To be human is to suffer!" He develops the idea further with this comment, "Because we are vulnerable and mortal, pain and anxiety are an integral part of our human existence."[1] I think he makes a very good point. None of us in our life can avoid the scourge of sickness or the pain of death. We are intensely affected by life around us. Just to exist is a struggle for many. For some people, to get through each day physically and mentally intact is an accomplishment. For others, not to go to bed hungry would be a blessing. Ultimately, everyone has to deal with personal tragedy. We are all touched at some point in life by suffering, such as divorce, accident, or serious illness. We are all potentially open to the touch of evil in various capacities, such as robbery, abuse, and even murder.

Sickness and disease are never easy to handle, but an ongoing, progressive illness is mentally, emotionally, and physically draining. When I made a marriage commitment that covered "in sickness and in health," I had no idea what that might entail. That promise has brought me to our present place of caring full-time for my wife, incapacitated by Parkinson's disease for the last twelve years. Taking care of her is all part of that commitment made more than half a century ago. How deeply one could wish things were different, but they are not, and we must push forward, not allowing circumstances to stifle the joy we derive from other aspects of life. We are, however, not alone. Our situation pales when we hear of others who suffer pain through tragic accidents and unexpected illnesses.

A friend of our son, who was in his forties, died recently from brain cancer. He was married with four children. I think of another friend whose son was in a coma for nine months from a serious car accident before he died. He too had a wife and two children at home. We have other friends whose son had cancer of both kidneys, discovered at his six-month medical examination. These are just in our own circle of friends. I am sure it is the same within your family and among your friends.

We live our lives with a mix of joy and contentment alongside suffering and pain. We delight in the joy of having children, but feel intense pain when they suffer. We face issues and deal with them the best way possible because we have no alternative. The pain is not always physical but often emotional. Our present position is where life has placed us. How do we deal with it? I believe we have to face it head-on and look at the causes of our discomfort.

WAS ALL THIS REALLY INTENDED?

I cannot believe that all this suffering was meant to be. I don't think that we were created simply to suffer. In the first two chapters of the Bible we read that whatever God made he "saw that it was good!" The human race was part of what was made good. And now we struggle. I don't believe that God intended for us to live a life of strife and struggle. Life is for us to enjoy and not just endure. Unfortunately, it is easier for us to see the downside and disadvantages of life than the upside and the potential within us.

In his book *Perseverance,* Tim Hague tells the story of his competing in and winning the very first Canadian television reality show, *The Amazing Race.* Nothing seemingly odd about that except that he suffers from the debilitating Parkinson's disease. Even to apply to compete in such a race would seem foolhardy. Hampered by his immobility issues, his was a story of endurance, determination, and perseverance. He ran the race partnered with his son Tim Jr., who exercised great love and patience in the midst of frustration as he supported his father mentally and physically. Together they pulled off a miracle.

Tim Hague writes, "Our lives are finite. We all know we've been given a certain number of days . . . Parkinson's has driven this reality home . . . It's a matter of being courageous enough to acknowledge the truth." He continues, "The options before us are limited only by our imagination and our willingness to dream new dreams."[2] Tim Hague is now in demand as a speaker around the world. His attitude has been an inspiration to many.

Not all of us face such severe obstacles as being born with one hand or contracting Parkinson's disease, but we all have to deal with issues in our lives that bring pain, stress, and sadness. It may be a breakdown of relationships among friends or acquaintances, or perhaps a serious occurrence of hostility within the family. It could be pain. It could be heartache. Innumerable life issues cause us unrelenting stress and discouragement.

Whatever you are going through right now, let me encourage you. We don't have to be prisoners of our circumstances. Be encouraged, because there is hope. Hope is a life saver. We cannot live without hope. With it, we have the potential to rise above anything that life throws at us. We can all find reasons to despair, but hope can eradicate despair and set us on a road to peace and fulfillment.

Maybe you have even felt like giving up; remember, never give up, there is always a solution. It's not always simple or even readily seen, but facing the issue is where we begin, and riding above it is where we want to be. We must refuse to be a victim of our circumstance. We need to take control of the situation, and through discipline and determination place ourselves out of the reach of those things that would crush our spirits. Consequently, our mindset is critical. A positive mindset can bring us to a place where we can overcome those frustrating and debilitating obstacles. I know each of our situations is different and peculiar to us, and the pain is real, but it is comforting to know that nothing, absolutely nothing, is insurmountable. There is always an answer and it's often closer than we think.

CHAPTER 2

When Life Seems Unfair

From our earliest days we all face inequalities. From team-choosing days on the school playground, to business environments in adulthood, we have all been in the position where someone has been favoured over us and we have thought to ourselves, "That's not fair!" Someone arrives late on the scene and gets a better deal. Someone joins the company after you and is promoted before you. Being overlooked or deliberately ignored can create negative thoughts about ourselves. We might begin to wonder, "What's wrong with me?"

Inexplicable things happen in life. You believe you are the right person for the job but you didn't get it. You believe your child should have been chosen for a particular part in the school play and she wasn't. Your son shines as an athlete but is not chosen to represent the school or the club. People make decisions the way they do for a myriad of reasons and often not in line with our thinking. Although the ability or giftedness might have been overlooked, it doesn't diminish those qualities or abilities. They remain. But we feel for our children and we feel hurt because of it. When we feel things are unfair and are left with an emotional hurt, or sadness from being let down, we are forced to find a way to deal with the situation.

When Camelia and Dmitry Moceanu from Illinois discovered their newborn little girl had no legs, they must have felt that life was totally unfair. Camelia did not even see her baby. Her husband felt she would not be able to handle it. The child was immediately given up for adoption. It took three months in a foster home where she was loved and cared for before being placed with her new adoptive parents, Sharon and Gerald Bricker. She was named Jennifer Bricker. Once Jen became old enough to know that she was different—she could have legitimately curled up in a corner, kept herself hidden from the world, and no one would have been any the wiser. However, that did not happen. In spite of her predicament, and encouraged by her new parents, she believed there were no limits to what she could achieve.

As a teenager, she went into gymnastics and won numerous awards. She did horseback riding and most other activities open to young people with no handicaps. Eventually Jen became an aerialist, performing at circuses around the world. She brought huge delight to the crowds and was a massive surprise to her family and friends. She then went on to become a well-known motivational speaker, travelling the world to share her message that nothing is impossible. Yet, in her attitude she is down to earth, humble, and aspires to impact everyone she meets. In her book *"Everything is Possible,"* she says that trusting God is her secret. At Jen's instigation, her biological parents had the opportunity to meet her and, understandably, were extremely proud of her achievements. I wonder if they ever questioned their actions in giving up their baby at birth. Far from turning out to be a massive burden, Jen Bricker turned into a living inspiration for thousands of people.[1]

Do you ever think life is unfair? Do you ever consider that life has dealt you a bad hand? When things go wrong and turn sour, do you think that the world is against you? It is true that life is often hard and things do go wrong. Our own daughter was only 5 lb. 7 oz. at birth and failed to gain weight as expected. We sensed something was wrong. Doctors discovered that she had a congenital heart problem that would require surgery to avoid an early death. At three months, she had the heart operation. The situation was corrected and she developed and grew as any other child. For us as young parents, however, those early months gave us great concern. Life has a habit of throwing obstacles at us which bring uncertainty and heartache.

Have you ever been terribly disappointed by something not working out, or a personal project that became a disaster, only to find out later that, if things had not happened the way they did, then the present situation would not have fallen into place or worked out as well as it has?

A friend of mine applied to serve overseas for a period of time in his profession. He put in his application to serve in Germany, only to be turned down. So the next year he did the same, with the same result. Shortly after the second refusal, his daughter came down with a serious medical condition. She needed a very specialized operation and treatment. It was available in the city in which they lived but it would not have been available abroad. Once his daughter was fully recovered, he applied again. This time his application was accepted and they enjoyed three years serving overseas. Was that coincidence or divine intervention?

One day during the 1980s my wife, Rita, went to see a medical specialist. He had been called out during the night on an emergency and told my wife that he was extremely tired. At the end of the appointment he wrote her a prescription for a drug, indicating a 300 mg strength in the medication instead of 30 mg. The pharmacist queried it with me, saying he had never seen such a high dosage, but he still went ahead and filled the prescription. My wife took the medication, and within twenty-four hours was walking into walls and doors, totally disoriented. She has always respected the authority of doctors and considered them experts in their field. Hence, she continued with the medication until persuaded otherwise. It had a long-term psychotic effect. It created a severe imbalance of brain chemicals. One doctor friend of ours said he was surprised it did not cause her to become violent. We suspect it contributed to her subsequent depressions.

Consequently, we are no strangers to the dark night of depression. If this is your experience we identify with you. Rita has had a number of bouts of severe depression, each one lasting approximately four months. Depression is insidious and diabolical, both for the sufferer and the caregiver. Feelings of isolation, abandonment, and hopelessness can cause endless hours of crying and despair. One becomes imprisoned in one's own house, with the caregiver sometimes unable even to leave the room. Depression is a serious matter and a deep pit from which to climb out. Climbing out is difficult, but with love, care, and patience it can be achieved.

Depressions can hit instantaneously, as with my wife, from traumatic events, such as hearing an adverse medical diagnosis or the loss of a loved one. For others, the road towards depression is more of a slow walk, strewn with times of loneliness, anxiety, negative views, adverse thoughts about oneself, low self-esteem, and a general sense that nobody cares. Either way, depression is devastating and emotionally very painful. The darkness is overwhelming. If you are being pulled down by depression, don't give up. There are people who love you and want to help.

Should we have felt that life was unfair because of the consequences from the overdose? Someone suggested we should sue. I believe that would have added enormous stress to our situation. We could have thought life was unfair, but there are times we have to make choices. For us to struggle with the rights and wrongs of our predicament would not have enhanced my wife's recovery. We are always subject to other people's fallibility and mistakes. That's life. That's how it is. We can do little to change circumstances, so we learn to accept them, whether fair or not.

Being human, we all have problems, some worse than others. I find it intriguing and encouraging when I read of those who have deliberately worked hard to overcome their inadequacies and disadvantaged position. Abraham Lincoln was elected the 16th president of the United States in 1860. Born in 1809 to farmer parents in Kentucky, he had less than 18 months of formal schooling. He was an avid reader and it was through reading that he made his way in life. He wanted to be a lawyer, so he privately read and studied law. He was admitted to the bar in 1837 at the age of 28. He started his political career in 1832 at the age of 23 and was elected President in 1860, some 28 years later, and began serving in January 1861. The civil war commenced in April of that year. He remained president until assassinated in April 1865.

He was thought of as one of the greatest presidents and leaders of his time. Lincoln was also a spiritual man who had a strong belief in God. But he was not without health problems. He suffered from severe migraine headaches and serious bouts of depression. It was not uncommon for him to spend days in bed recovering from these maladies. Yet his achievements in the government, military, and civil arenas were superb. For a man who had little formal education, faced innumerable obstacles in pursuing a political career while dealing with ongoing difficulties, his lifetime accomplishments were outstanding. No one knows what more he might have achieved had he not had his life taken from him at age 56. Was life unfair to him? Maybe, but he certainly did not allow it to deter him from making a valuable contribution to the world around him.

Other leaders like him had reasons to think that life was unfair. Winston Churchill overcame extreme learning disabilities to lead the United Kingdom during the Second World War. Franklin D. Roosevelt overcame polio and paralysis and became the longest serving president of the United States. Looking at the lives of such people should help us put our problems into perspective. These were ordinary people like you and me. They simply refused to allow their disadvantages to dominate or rule their lives. With determination and resolve they saw beyond the present into the possibilities of the future. To overcome was their intent, and they succeeded. We too can have the same intent and be determined to rise above our situations.

Life happens, and it is not always pretty, and we humans are known for putting on a brave face. We try to convey to the world that everything is fine. We put on a mask to hide the hurt, the pain, and the embarrassment of our situation. We are reluctant openly to expose our wounds. Why do we try to hide the truth? Often the things that go wrong are out of our control. Yet we are left with emotional pain and heartache. We legitimately think that life is unfair. How do we deal with this kind of pressure? How do we overcome this emotional storm?

Sadly, and regrettably, some give up or turn to substance abuse or other addictions in an attempt to numb the devastating feelings. While this approach may seem to help for a time, the ultimate effect is usually disastrous. Some turn to faith in God. Looking at life through the perspective of our faith helps to give us a balanced view. It helps us see beyond today to the brighter prospect of tomorrow. As God's children, learning that he cares for us, is in control, and has our interest at heart, provides comfort and confidence in our trials. What is the point of having a faith if we cannot trust God to handle our difficult situations? If you are going through an emotional low, be encouraged because there is always a solution. You will come through this.

Isaiah 61 is a wonderful section in the Bible that talks about God turning ashes into beauty and turning a spirit of despair into praise. It is a superb picture of God turning the ashes of hurt and disappointment into the beauty of rejoicing and gladness! Some people indicate that if it had not been for their adversity, they would not have known the beautiful moments of healing, and experienced the serenity of God's peace. God is in the business of taking the adverse and turning it into something good. God can turn the ugly into joy and beauty. It seems that when bad things happen they often lead us into a good place.

When Karyn Buxman's son was 13 years old, he began having bouts of excruciating pain in his head, causing him to scream. This would be followed by a burning sensation in his feet, and finally he would be paralyzed from the neck down for about an hour. This took place several times a day. Consulting many doctors and specialists brought no answer. The episodes continued. While Karyn was trying to find a solution for this, another son called her from college. He had experienced pain in his chest and had gone to the emergency at the local hospital, where they found a fist-sized lump in his chest. It was cancer. Also during this period, her mother was diagnosed with Alzheimer's. At the same time, she was going through a divorce. It is incredible what the mind can tolerate. Amazingly she survived the onslaught. She persevered and came out the other side, sane. The first son's nasty experience lasted seven years but disappeared as mysteriously as it had arrived. The second son had an operation and went through chemotherapy on his road to recovery.

Karyn is a well-known public speaker in the United States, and listening to her story the sentence that stood out to me was, "The best things in my life have come from the most difficult times!" She had to go through the storm to know and appreciate the calm and peace that followed. I believe this was one of those times when God turned ashes into beauty, and what he did for Karyn he can do for you and for me.

CHAPTER 3

Order out of Chaos

Billingsgate Fish Market in the city of London received its charter to trade in fish in 1699. The market is still operational, and if you go there around 4:30 in the morning on any business day you would find many men in their long rubber aprons lifting boxes of fish, moving them around on carts, going in all directions. To the untrained eye, it looks overly busy and chaotic. Yet by 8:30 a.m. the market is closed and thousands of pounds of fish have changed hands and are on their way to their final destinations all over the country. The underlying system does its job, and out of the seeming chaos of noise and busyness comes order. Order is often birthed in chaos.

When I was a pay clerk in the British Army, I worked with a sergeant who was a neat freak. I am not sure how many times a week he would clear everything off his desk, wipe it down, and put the papers back in a neat pile. Most of us get to the point where suddenly we get a similar urge, so we decide to clean up a room. For me it is my study. I dust the books and generally make the room presentable and the desk top more workable. It is amazing how good one feels after it is done. I believe there is a universal principle that humankind prefers order rather than chaos. Although I understand that genius goes along with untidiness—I like to think so—I would assume that even a genius likes some semblance of order in his or her life.

I think as humans we generally desire organization and structure. We love everything to be in order, everything right at home, at school, and at work. We love it when everything ticks along smoothly without stress and conflict. In our minds, everything has its place and we like it when everything is in its place. It makes us feel good. We feel comfortable. Order provides stability for us. Unfortunately, life is not always orderly. Chaos does affect our lives at times. It hits us when things go wrong. We are thrust into chaos when we are sideswiped by an unexpected crisis in life. Physical and mental chaos disturbs many of us.

Have you ever considered just how orderly the natural world is? There are ecological patterns in plant, animal, and sea life. There are growth patterns and food chains that operate seamlessly. Everything seems to have its place, knows its place, and usually keeps within those pre-ordained boundaries.

I think of bird migration flying thousands of miles to warmer climates and returning every year. The monarch butterflies do the same. They fly 4000 miles in their migration pattern to Mexico. Whales do a similar thing, travelling four thousand miles to warmer waters to have their young. I think of the spawning habits of salmon and how, after three years, and some after four years in the ocean, they return to their place of birth to spawn another generation. Such examples just scratch the surface of the intricacies of the plant and animal kingdom, the epitome of order. Creation brought structure and order.

Sadly, we find that we live in world where chaos seems to reign supreme. It is anything but a settled and peaceful place. Protestations and military conflict affect virtually all continents. So many countries are embroiled in internal rebellious strife or political turmoil. Terrorist activity occurs almost anywhere on the globe. Millions are dying from starvation. Ebola, cholera, and other viruses are taking their toll and growing in intensity. Millions of refugees are displaced, many through ethnic cleansing. Crime increases, with mass shootings and murder high on the list. Suicide is at an all-time high. Such is the despair of thousands. This is not a pretty picture of our world. It is a world full of chaos.

I wonder if we have become so acclimatized to such a global picture that it no longer carries any shock value. We hear the news and then unthinkingly switch to another channel. Perhaps we sense that it does not affect us and we have to accept it for what it is. It is not that we don't care about the suffering, deprivation, and inhumane situations around the world, but that we feel helpless and unable to do much about it. But even as spectators, I don't believe we can be totally unmoved by what we read and hear. It is our world and we all are part of it. We must never see people just as numbers instead of human beings who live, think, sleep, and love just as we do, but who do so in the midst of devastation.

OUR PERSONAL CHAOS

In our personal world, I think we try hard to have order and avoid chaos. When things go well we can be on top of the world, but when things are not right it is disturbing and often painful. Life hurts when broken or severed relationships litter our pathway or when we experience heartache from disappointments. Often we are confused as to why or how something went wrong or how we ended up in the current difficult situation. Misunderstandings occur regularly. Harsh words leave indelible scars and create emotional stress. Even off the cuff, mindless comments can bring irreparable damage. Then when we want to put things right we find ourselves procrastinating and leave the wounds open and festering. Yet, like physical wounds, emotional healing is available with proper care and treatment, even if it hurts to treat it. The good thing is that these situations can be corrected. Relationships can be healed. Emotional turmoil can be calmed.

Even if outwardly everything seems to be in order, yet inwardly we may still suffer from mental chaos. I am not referring to mental illness but rather being mentally distraught, overloaded, and disturbed from the stress and pressures of life. It is something we are often reluctant to admit. Our business life, our home life, our school life, and even our social lives bring mental stresses and strains that are hard to handle. Worry is a killer. We know that 95% of things that cause worry never occur, but that doesn't stop some people being enslaved to worry. Finances, work, health, parents, children, relationships, and marriage are all contenders for normal and abnormal worry. Unrelenting anxiety about the future or the "what ifs" of life can be paralyzing.

It is true that we cannot go through life unconcerned about situations but concern and worry are worlds apart. Usually, concern is level-headed thinking, while worry seems to have little structure. Concern considers what solutions might be available, whereas worry sees the problem as overwhelming. Usually the worrier lives in hope that the situation will change or go away. Worrying is often accompanied or caused by negativity. Under such conditions life appears to present an insurmountable challenge.

Stress, on the other hand, although a cousin to worry, is more definable. The story is told of a psychology professor who held up a glass of water and asked the class how much they thought the glass of water weighed. She received answers up to a couple of pounds. The professor then said, "From my perspective the absolute weight of this glass is irrelevant. It all depends on how long I hold it!" She went on to explain that holding it for a minute or two it would be light. To hold it for an hour the arm would ache and for a day the arm would cramp and become paralyzed. She said, "The longer I hold it the heavier it feels to me." She then continued, "Your worries, frustrations, disappointments, and stressful thoughts are very much like this glass of water. Think about them a little while and nothing happens. If you think about them longer you begin to feel noticeable pain. Think about them all day long and you can become numb and paralyzed, incapable of doing anything else until you drop them."

We deal with the normal stresses of everyday life, usually with helpful results. These cause no long-term problem and build our character and resolve in dealing with daily life. Some stresses, however, coming from things outside of our control, if left alone, can degenerate into mental chaos. Worse than that, constant stress will result in adverse health conditions. The immediate symptoms include an increase in blood pressure, a racing pulse, sweating, faster breathing, and muscle tension, while the longer-term affects can be pain in the chest or back, stomach problems, anger, irritability, headaches, and if left untreated can lead to a heart attack or stroke. Such is the seriousness of ongoing stress.

We need to avoid stress as much as possible, although it is impossible to do so totally. In fact, just as our physical muscles need tension, so our minds need manageable stress. The key is to find the balance between productive and unhelpful stress. We know that life must go on. Things have to be done. Life has to be lived in and outside the family. Work must proceed. The monthly income must be in the bank. Responsibilities must be fulfilled. Your boss, your spouse, and your children all bring to bear a certain amount of pressure and expectation, and rightly so. Each has a place in your life and you have an obligation to them. Those within the family usually look for your counsel, your advice, and your support. Rest comes only at a premium. What then is the answer to mental chaos? How do we get order out of such chaos?

CONTEMPLATION IS EFFECTIVE

Do you ever just sit back, close your eyes and just think? Do you ever spend time in honest-to-goodness quiet reflection? Although meditation in various forms has become quite a popular activity over the last decade or so, I am not talking about sitting cross-legged and repeating some mantra. I am talking about taking time out to review your life. Seriously to consider where you have come from, the influence on you from your peers and from life in general, as well as the upbringing provided by your parents. Do you ever consider what you have gone through, good and bad, and then look at where you are today? It's a worthwhile exercise. By doing so you can begin to weigh the good against the bad, the positive against the negative. You begin to realize how many things have gone right as opposed to going wrong.

We may still hurt from various mishaps, some bruises, or abrasions from minor life skirmishes, but we notice how they have healed over time. We can also see how less important they have become as the pain has subsided. We gradually gain a better perspective on life. The important issues rise to the top and we begin to focus on them – relationships, family, friends, colleagues, and acquaintances. They all play their part in the life we lead. All affect us in some way.

Give some time to private solitude and you will be surprised how much happier you feel about yourself. Unfortunately, we see the negative aspects of ourselves more readily than the positive, which is a shame. We make a mistake or two along the way and come down on ourselves as though we fail in everything. It is never an all-or-nothing situation. We must accept the mistakes and the failures but also recognize the successes.

Sometimes it takes input from others to help recognize the valuable contribution we may have made to those around us. We are taught to be humble, but what does that mean? It certainly does not mean belittling ourselves and thinking less of ourselves than we should. I have heard humility described as "an honest view of ourselves." I believe there is a balance between humility and being confident or self-assured. That should be our aim. Looking honestly in the mirror will reveal both sides of the coin. A daily quiet reflective period will do wonders to change mental chaos to calmness and order. It allows the mind to get things in a proper, balanced perspective. Even corporations are encouraging management to take out special moments to breathe and relax. Doctors are also recommending it for patients who need to get on top of stress.

Reflection—or contemplation—is different for each of us. What I am suggesting here is more than just a five-minute break from the busyness of the day. Life goes by so fast and we live at such a tremendous pace that we forget to slow down and take in the scenery. I understand that meditation, prayer, or simple reflection have a positive effect upon the frontal cortex of the brain. It helps to decrease stress and relieve anxiety. Both mind and body benefit enormously from such a small exercise. It makes sense to set aside a special time for quietness and contemplation.

What do you concentrate on during those times? What do you meditate on? What do you think about? Reflect upon yourself, your life, your spouse, your family, and those around you. Think about where you have been and hopefully where you are heading. Don't be shy to think about what you have achieved and be pleased about it. Think about the positive aspects of your life. Consider where you have made a valuable contribution to someone else's life. Also think about what or who has made a valuable contribution to your life. It could be people, a book, or even a special event. This brings a sense of gratitude and thankfulness which builds positive thinking.

It's hard to be grateful and unhappy at the same time. It is difficult to be grateful and depressed at the same time. Reflection quiets the mind, recharges our spiritual and emotional batteries, and allows God to deal with issues in our lives. Some religions provide specific instructions to follow. For the Christian, meaningful times of meditation obviously include Bible reading and prayer. These are essential exercises in spiritual meditation. To dwell on your relationship with God and gratefulness for the blessings received will lift your spirit.

Quiet contemplation will help you rise above the noise and chaos around you. It will help you arrive at the place where you are happy with yourself and content with your situation. Take the time to make it happen. You'll be glad you did.

CHAPTER 4

Our Thinking Is Critical

In January 2019, Lee Roebeck found herself, on the streets of Johannesburg in South Africa, surrounded by four gun-wielding kidnappers, who manhandled her into the trunk of a car. She was driven around for three hours. She had no idea the reason for this. Incredibly, and ironically, Lee had recently taken a course in which she learned that the control of your thinking is critical in all situations. Remembering what she had learned, instead of panicking, she was determined, and able, to keep control of her mind. She took courage by thinking about Viktor Frankl and his positive attitude while he was a prisoner in a concentration camp. He emphasized that we can always choose what we think, regardless of our circumstance.

As Lee began to take charge of her thoughts, she gradually calmed down emotionally. She thanked God that her four-year-old was not with her at the time of the kidnapping. She then began to pray for her kidnappers and for their families. She prayed that they would change their lives and find a way to make a difference in the world. As she did all this in her mind she became surprisingly calm and remained in total control of her senses. At the end of the three hour ordeal she was released unharmed, none the wiser for why she was kidnapped. Possibly a mistaken identity. How glad she was that she had learned to control her thinking. Lee proved that it really is our choice as to what we think.

The mind is powerful. It is stronger than we might think. Consider the humble placebo. In his fascinating book *"You are the Placebo,"* Dr. Joe Dispenza deals extensively with studies on the effectiveness of placebos.[1] It would appear that the very act of taking a tablet causes a psychological reaction, often giving a positive result to the well-being of the patient. Even when people have known they were being given a placebo, the results have often been positive, which is difficult to understand. But there is no question that placebos work, not because of their content, but purely from the mind believing that medication is being ingested. As far back as the middle of the last century it was known that people recovered from their illnesses while being treated with a sugar pill or even fake surgery. The mind causes the body to respond positively and bring about changes from the body's own defense mechanism. It literally is mind over matter.

WE ARE WHAT WE THINK?

Our thinking directly affects our activity. Who we are in our mind is displayed through our action. The mind gives direction to the brain, which in turn instructs the body. As an aside, have you ever wondered where the mind is? Well, it seems that it is certainly not in a neat little box in the middle of the brain. When people say, "My mind is all over the place," they speak the truth more than they probably know. Although the hippocampus stores long-term memories, it would appear that fragments of knowledge relating to the same events and conversations can be found in various places in the brain. Thus, when we recall memories it is not uncommon for different pieces from similar occurrences to become entangled, making our memories not quite so genuine and authentic as we might assume. But I digress.

Our feelings are determined by our thinking. If we are feeling elated, it has come from some good news or pleasant events. If we are feeling sad or down, it may well be because of thoughts of disappointing or disturbing news. Feeling angry is our reaction to something that has upset us. It is not the occurrence itself but our response to it that matters. Our thinking is crucial to how we feel. Our actions also are in direct correlation to our thinking. Because our mind exerts power over our bodies, our behaviour is greatly influenced by our self-image and how we see life.

Healthy thinking leads to healthy living. Every action is preceded by a thought process. Our thinking predisposes us to accomplishments or failure. Negative thinking creates negative patterns. Positive thinking creates positive patterns. Those patterns etched in the brain determine what we do. Apparently, Aristotle once said, "We are what we repeatedly do." The largest influence as to who we are, and what we are, comes from the mind.

Our thinking can even influence the state of our health. It is common knowledge that so many diseases are aggravated or caused by stress, worry, and anxiety, all of which originate in the mind. The effects trickle down through the brain and contribute to adverse conditions in the body. In fact, some have suggested that as much as 87% of illnesses can be attributed to our thoughts, while the remaining 13% can be blamed on genetics, our diet, and our toxic environment. Like me, you probably know people who exude negative sentiment. One such lady I know seemingly finds everything wrong with life and people around her. Nothing ever appears to go right. Her attitude continuously expresses such sentiment. I have to wonder whether her severe arthritic condition is not directly related to years of negativity. The body listens and responds to what the mind tells it. What we have entertained and fed our mind creates our demeanor. We become what we think.

Thinking is probably the most critical and important aspect of our lives because, as indicated, it dictates and controls our behaviour. In her book *"Think, Learn, Succeed,"* Dr. Caroline Leaf emphasizes the overriding necessity for having a correct mindset. Our mindset determines our action. It gives direction to our thought patterns, which in turn causes us to make choices. Those choices formulate our behaviour and lifestyle. Dr. Leaf describes what a mindset is: "A mindset is an attitude, or a cluster of thoughts with attached information and emotions that generate a particular perception. They shape how you see and interact with the world. They can catapult you forward, allowing you to achieve your dreams, or put you in reverse drive if you are not careful. A mindset is therefore a significant mental resource and source of power."[2] Such is the importance of establishing a correct mindset. It seems that without it we will flounder in a sea of indecisive action or go wandering down the wrong track.

Another interesting view on mindset comes from the very popular book, *Mindset,* by Dr. Carol S. Dweck.[3] She puts forward the concept that there are predominantly two mindsets, the fixed and the growth mindsets. The first says that the intelligence you were born with is what stays with you, whereas the growth mindset continues to acquire more intelligence as your knowledge increases throughout life. The fixed mindset is limiting in its scope of accomplishments, while the growth mindset is more outgoing as it continues to seek new avenues in its desire to develop greater understanding and acquire more knowledge while investigating new vistas of life. Our mindsets hold a big influence over what we do and in what we achieve. Control our thinking and we can control our actions.

Interestingly, Sonia Ricotti says in her book *Unsinkable,* "You can be confronted with challenging circumstances that make it seem as though everything is falling apart all around you, and still experience true inner peace and joy. You can also have everything going well in your life and yet be unhappy, stressed, and have your mind filled with chaos and dissatisfaction."[4] What's the difference? It is the mind. It is the mindset. Have a balanced mindset and you will be able to control the influence external events and other people have upon you.

To whom do we talk most in life? Ourselves, of course. We are constantly talking to ourselves silently and persuasively. What we say is based mostly upon how we see ourselves, and subsequently, how others see us. We follow the inner voice and display the thought patterns we have constructed for good or bad. What we tell ourselves about ourselves is very important.

Self-talk has the inordinate ability to build or destroy character, because our subconscious or unconscious mind has no choice but to believe what we tell it. Self-talk is critical regarding our self-esteem. Robert Collier, an American writer from early last century, said, "One comes to believe whatever one repeats to oneself." Just as our thinking matters, so does our self-talk. Our self-talk and self-view feed upon each other. What we think about ourselves becomes reality. Everything we say and think has consequences, especially upon ourselves. We should think long about that last sentence.

All of us carry a picture of ourselves within our mind's eye and quietly and surreptitiously we feed ourselves with the essence of that picture. A lack of self-esteem will result from a constant barrage of negative thoughts, such as, "I am not very good," or "I have never achieved much in my life," or "I'm a failure," and so on. Repeating such statements internally will destroy our sense of worth. However, remember this, the negative picture we create of ourselves is often false and rarely has basis in reality. It has been built on erroneous information as we have concentrated on our failures or shortcomings or maybe comments from others who are uninformed of all aspects of our real self. Unfortunately, we so readily believe the negative suggestions. It is amazing that if we hear several compliments about us and then one nasty criticism, what do we dwell on and remember? It is the negative comment. We need to rid ourselves of any negative self-image we carry. As we change our thinking, we will change our sense of worth.

For good or bad, we convey to others what we think of ourselves. Our speech, our deportment, our attitude, and body language tell a story. In some cases, even how we dress gives an indication of how we view ourselves. Other people read us better than we might think. It is important that we think well of ourselves so that others will do the same.

Generalizations are also most unhelpful. For instance, if something is not right it does not mean that everything is wrong. If a job interview, or two, achieves nothing there is no reason to think, "I will never be able to get a job." Belittling oneself and refusing to recognize personal achievements is counter-productive. It lays the groundwork for failure and depression. Negative statements like, "I never seem to do things right," or "I always seem to say the wrong thing," add fuel to the destruction of our self-image. Have you noticed how negative statements to the mind become reality? Is it surprising that when we say, "I knew it would be a bad week," it turns out just that way? Or when we say, "I knew it would go wrong," and it did. These statements become self-fulfilling. It is what the mind was expecting and therefore it happened.

THE IMPORTANCE OF FEELING GOOD ABOUT OURSELVES

We need to feel good about ourselves. I do not mean a self-inflated, unrealistic display of arrogance, but a demeanor of quiet confidence that all is well. We need good self-esteem. We need to think well of ourselves. How do we do that? First, we need to understand that we are no different from those around us. None of us is perfect. We all have our struggles, inwardly and externally. Even those who appear to be doing well in life have or have had struggles. We compare ourselves with others in the hope that we compare favourably. But life is not a question of living in comparison to others. We look at others and think they have it all together. We assume they have life all neatly packaged. We have no idea of their internal conflict or even their struggle with self-image.

The way to change our own self-image is to begin filling our minds with positive self-talk statements. We need to change the "I can't" to "I can if I put my mind to it." We need to tell ourselves, "It may take some effort, but I know I can do this." We need to see the success of others and think, "If they can do it, so can I." We need to recognize our long-term achievements and not dwell on the momentary failures. We all fail at various points but we have to pick ourselves up and press on regardless, because life is bigger than a temporary failure.

Take a moment, check back through your life and think of the numerous things you have successfully achieved. Think of schooling and graduation. Think about your first job or other positions you have had and think about your marriage and your children. Think of the good input you have had into other people's lives as you have walked the journey of life. You have done things that no one else could, because only you were found in that place at that moment. I believe that we each have a purpose for being here, ordained and orchestrated by God. You have a proven purpose for being here. No one else can take your place. No one else can fill your shoes. No one else can do the job that you are called to do. You are unique and uniquely suited to your purpose. How can you feel anything else but needed and important?

The objective is to live as only you can. You alone can be the outward expression of who you are. Putting yourself down and thinking less of yourself than you should not only does yourself a great disservice, but it limits your opportunity to share who you really are and in what capacity you fit. We all fit in somewhere. We are unique and we are uniquely different. You are different from me as I am from you, and that was intentional. Our differences are complementary. Our differences build and support each other.

Imagine if we were all cookie-cutter robots. How boring and uniform life would be. That is not how it is. There is a delightful distinction between us, yet there is a compelling sameness in our needs and aspirations. We complement each other. What you can do I cannot do because it is you and your individual abilities that fit your chosen position or situation. We are not accidents of parental biology. We are not the result of fate. We are here as God intended—unique, purposeful beings.

If we have issues from the past that are causing us self-conceptual problems in the present, we need to dig them out and change the pattern of thinking. It will take much honesty and humility to search for those false beliefs that have plagued our minds for years. Don't be surprised to experience similar sentiments and feelings associated with the original event. Keep digging until you discover the original source of your negative thinking. What were you told that sent you down the wrong path? Expose it for what it is, a lie! Face it, then walk away from it. Turn your back on it and refuse to let it tie you down and hold you back any longer. Negative thinking is a choice. I like to believe that our default system is optimism, recognizing the best in life. I believe that God wants our lives to be purposeful, contented, happy, and abundant. A life that is exciting, fulfilling, and meaningful to oneself and those around.

Maybe it will take some deliberate changing, refreshing, or renewing of our minds to get us into a better place. The renewing or changing of our minds is no simple self-talk trick. It means coming to grips with the deeply-engraved patterns that have been etched in our minds for years. With every thought, new neural pathways are established. Repetitious thoughts cause those pathways to deepen. Constant thoughts become deeply entrenched patterns within the brain. If they are negative thoughts about ourselves, other people, or the world in general, then those negative thoughts turn into negative patterns that dictate our moods and attitude, bringing with them feelings of discontent and depression.

SUMMING UP

Renewing of the mind means a deliberate act of changing those negative patterns and replacing them with positive thoughts. We all have that capacity. We choose what we think. We choose our focus. Not necessarily those fleeting thoughts that enter our heads and disappear almost immediately, but the thoughts we choose to dwell on. If our thought patterns are doing us no favours, then we must change them. It takes desire and discipline to set such a change in motion. It takes determination and motivation. We have to uproot the old tracks and lay down new ones. God brought us into this world as intelligent, worthy, deserving human beings with the ability to think independently. Let's not waste that ability.

Start each day with a clean slate. Rid yourself of the weight of negative thoughts. Replace them with positive, uplifting thoughts that carry joy and optimism for the future. Today is a new day. What you think today will affect tomorrow and the day after that and so on. Don't delay, put in place now a positive mindset which will propel you into the future with confidence and will give you assurance that life can be better and will be better. Your thinking can take you there.

CHAPTER 5

Our Attitude Says It All

Nine-year-old Ezra Finch was born with one leg missing and only one finger on one hand. They took the big toe from his foot and made him another finger and gave him a prosthetic leg. If you watched him play soccer you would not know of his disability except for the visible artificial leg. He concentrates rather on his ability to perform. I heard him interviewed. He displayed an incredibly mature attitude. He said, "I am so grateful to have a great family, great legs, great friends, a great school, and a great life." He admitted that life brings many challenges, but he tries to knock down the wall of challenges. He continued, "I think about what I have instead of what I don't have." He concluded the interview with, "It was a good thing to be born like this!" Remarkable statements from a remarkable young boy. What an incredible attitude! An attitude of gratitude goes such a long way in overcoming life's obstacles.

In his book *The Laws of Human Nature,* Robert Green discusses the life of Anton Chekov, the well-known Russian writer and playwright.[1] Born in a small Russian village in abject poverty, he and his four brothers and sisters were regularly beaten by their father, who indicated it was what God wanted to keep them humble. The father owned a small grocery store, but through mismanagement and drunkenness the outstanding bills became more than could be paid. Two of his sons had earlier moved to Moscow to get away from their father, but now he followed them to avoid creditors. His wife tried unsuccessfully to run the business but it was too far gone and went into bankruptcy. A boarder and so-called friend tried to help her manage her financial affairs, only to swindle her out of her own house. She too went with her other two children to Moscow. Anton stayed to finish his schooling and was given a small corner of one room in their original house. He studied hard and worked as a private tutor to pay for his meals.

Life was very hard. Spending three years alone, away from family, he blamed his father for his situation and became quite bitter and depressed. However, those years gave him time to gain a greatly improved perspective on life. He tried to find reasons for the plight of his family and why his father was as he was. He realized that what the father had inflicted upon the family was based upon his upbringing. His father had been born into a life of serfdom and had been beaten by his father. It was therefore what he knew and acted accordingly.

While considering all this, Anton quite suddenly had an overwhelming sense of love and forgiveness for his father. Having finished his schooling, he went to Moscow and joined his family, whom he discovered were living in terrible conditions in one room in a basement tenement. At nineteen years of age he took charge of the situation. He found work for himself, managed to get a job for his father, enrolled his brothers back into school, and eventually moved the family into their own apartment. The transformation of his heart and his attitude of mind changed the whole family scenario. His thinking had changed. His attitude had changed. His positivity lifted the family out of their extremely unpleasant circumstances to a more acceptable standard of living.

ATTITUDE IS EVERYTHING

Thinking and attitude are closely aligned. Attitude is the external expression of our internal thinking. Our attitude to life has been built on the process and concepts we hold in our minds from the perceptions we have made through our life experience. I once read that "attitude is everything" and I have come to understand why the writer said that. People we meet respond to us according to the attitude we portray to them. If we are positive and upbeat in social settings, then we will mostly get that treatment in return. The opposite is also true. Face the world with a negative and depressed demeanor and others will reflect that back to you or will avoid you altogether. It affects how we see the world, how we see other people, and how we interpret events and situations. We will see the world either in an optimistic and agreeable manner or we will see everything with pessimistic eyes and find life generally disagreeable.

At the board meeting of a charity, two people were given the same task, to find some volunteer helpers to assist on a project. One mentally objected with the "why me" syndrome and went home determined that she knew no one who would volunteer. The other immediately began to think of which friends would be open to volunteering and began contacting them as soon as she arrived home. It was simply a self-fulfilling exercise. Things work out according to our expectation and attitude. The attitude made the difference. Enthusiasm, which is an attitude, is often infectious.

Our attitude to life, to people, to work, to family, and to friends is critical. It's often the difference between enduring or enjoying life. We may not think too much about our attitude, but it affects all situations that bring us in touch with people. Our attitude reflects what is going on inside but is seen on the outside. What people see on the outside is all that people have to read who we are. The attitude says it all. How do we come across to people? Do we have a critical spirit or do we have a pleasant and accepting attitude? Do we portray ourselves as judgmental or do we show an encouraging spirit? Do we have a jealous streak in us? Do we look enviously at what others have, often portraying an attitude that we have been left out or left behind, always wishing things were different, never satisfied with what we have, always thinking there is more or should be more? If we do, then we are not helping ourselves.

A dangerous attitude is that of judging one another. This can unexpectedly come back to bite us. How often do we assume things about others that turn out to be incorrect? We make judgement calls without having the full facts. We are all different. We all have obstacles, difficulties, struggles, and brick walls to face. Mostly we are unaware of the real position other people find themselves in. We have no idea of the battle they might be fighting, which they conveniently hide from us. They could be struggling with all kinds of personal or relational issues. Our wrong assumptions can be hurtful. We may be different but our needs are the same. We want to be loved, accepted, and understood. We are the beneficiaries if we replace criticism with love and understanding.

Comparing ourselves to others is a common practice that seems to ignore our unique differences. We come from different backgrounds, upbringing, and schooling, and have different occupations. Our DNA and fingerprints are uniquely different. Our life's journey has been different from others. We look different, think differently, act differently, hold different views on life, and have unique preferences. It makes no sense to compare ourselves with others. None of us has travelled the same road. Because of those differences we make, and have made, different choices. Those choices led to different lifestyles, different roads, different careers, and hence, different achievements. If we want to do any comparison we should be doing it with ourselves. How do we stack up today as opposed to our yesterday?

When we struggle financially, it is not uncommon to wish that we had what others have and that our life would run as smoothly as theirs. Again, we are looking only on the outside. We have no idea how smooth or rough their life really is. We look at the lovely house and the nice car. We see them as a well-groomed family with good jobs and suspected good income. We see them as having it all together, and life appears wonderful. But we have no idea of what is happening inside. They may have internal, hidden pain, or they might be suffering extraordinary discord with their spouse or children. They may be struggling to keep everything looking good to the outside world. Our envy may be totally misplaced. We are probably only causing ourselves unnecessary angst and it does nothing to improve our own situation.

How much healthier and better for us, and others, if we display an attitude of kindness and generosity! If we ignore what others appear to have and seem to be enjoying, and concentrate on displaying an attitude of optimism and positivity. If we show a spirit of appreciation and gratefulness, others around us will benefit. It tends to be contagious and spreads like ripples on a pond. If we act as though we got out on the wrong side of the bed, or like the proverbial bear with the sore head, how can people warm up to us? We need to be people whom others enjoy being around. We need to be those who can lift the spirits of other people just by being with them. We benefit along with others when we convey a positive and congenial attitude.

OUR SELF-VIEW IS IMPORTANT

One of my first occupations after leaving school was working at the London Stock Exchange. I well remember working shoulder to shoulder with others whose education far exceeded mine. In fact, most had attended private school. It was quite intimidating. However, I decided that I would not let my lack of education hinder me from learning the business and showing that I could do the work. I enjoyed the job, which helped me put in the time and effort to succeed. I could have adopted the attitude that I would not be able to compete in such an environment, and moved on. That would have demonstrated a losing attitude and resulted in unnecessarily putting myself down. As it turned out, I worked hard, proved my competence, and became a respected member of the team.

We may have adopted a view of ourselves or an attitude that can be inherently destructive. I am talking about the self-view that says, "I am not worthy." or "I am not deserving," or "I am just not good enough." Such statements are self-limiting and encourage us to believe that we can never compare to others in tasks or achievements. Such negative sentiments are self-fulfilling, and sadly, we unconsciously accept them as truth instead of the lies they prove to be.

Some believe that such a self-view or attitude can be generational in origin, as with the father of Anton

Chekov. Although I can see how easily mistreatment to one generation can be passed on to another, I tend to believe that such a negative view of oneself is birthed more during a child's early development years. During those early, impressionable years, children tacitly pick up parental or adult attitudes, whether spoken or not. A child under three years of age can be emotionally damaged quite unwittingly by an angry parent overreacting to some small misdemeanor. The child reads the face and hears the anger in the voice and interprets it as "I am not loved!" It takes very few such outbursts to solidify a long-term negative sense within the child.

As an illustration, how many children have picked up that sex was a taboo subject, not to be talked about or discussed? This then created an unhealthy and even unnatural interest in the subject or allowed the child to go into the world with a skewed view that sex is to be avoided. This imbalanced view of sex haunts the person for years, maybe life. It affects relationships and is the scourge of many marital conflicts. Wrong or misinformed attitudes from parents or teachers passed on can have devastating results.

Picture this not uncommon scenario. A child at the dinner table says, "I think I want to become a doctor," or some other prominent professional. A member of the family remarks, "Oh yes, just like I wanted to become Prime Minister," inferring that the child has little chance of achieving such a position. Far worse is to be told directly, "You will never make anything of yourself," which is usually added unthinkingly to a remark about not having done homework. That would be enough for some children to adopt a negative attitude about themselves and carry it for years to their own detriment. Their view of themselves and possibilities are now limited and fixed. This is a tragedy because mostly it is a false supposition and sets the child on the wrong track. They think far less of themselves than they need to or should.

Parents carry a heavy weight of responsibility in shaping their children's mental picture of themselves. They can offer a tremendous positive influence in the child's development or they can do irreparable damage simply by their attitude. Hence it is not uncommon for some of us to carry for years the effects of being at the wrong end of such a negative attitude. It may not have been parents, but teachers or work colleagues who brought about the hurt. These buried events have their way of staying with us or catching up with us somewhere along our journey.

During times of discouragement, of sadness, and maybe even depression, we think back and remember the hurts of yesterday as they rise to the surface. Maybe some occurrence of long ago has stayed with us and has influenced our thinking and consequently our moods and perhaps even our self-view. It is amazing how a nasty comment, an open criticism, or an unhelpful inference can create so much mental turmoil. If that is the case, we need to find it, recognize it, face it, and release ourselves from it. Doing so will set us on the road to new vistas and new horizons.

If this is you, then know this. You no longer need to have your life subjected to some past unfounded and untrue criticism. You can face it and shake it. It may require you to forgive someone for what they said or did, but in doing so you will be the one released from the prison or bondage that has weighed upon you and maybe held you back for years. You will feel like a caged bird suddenly released to take off and fly to places in your life where you have longed to be. You will find fresh impetus to do things that you have constantly put on the back burner. It will give you motivation to reach for new things you once considered unavailable. If you change your mind and your attitude, the world will change around you.

If ever there was a classic case of an attitude changing the world, it is in the story of *A Christmas Carol*. When Scrooge had experienced the visits from the three Christmas ghosts in his dream, he awoke to find he had a second chance to put things right. His attitude did a 180 degree turn. Nothing in the world had changed, yet for Scrooge everything had changed. His attitude to people and to life itself changed and the whole world changed with it. People came to think well of him. He himself moved from being dour, miserable, and miserly to being open, generous, and pleasant.

A far more recent example of choosing the right attitude comes from a young man from Texas. Jerry Long was 17 when, through a diving accident, he became paralyzed from the neck down. He learned to type with a mouth stick. He took courses from a local community college through the use of a special telephone which also allowed him to participate in classroom discussions. He was determined to win over his situation. At that time he wrote a letter to Viktor Frankl in which he stated "I view my life as being abundant with meaning and purpose. The attitude that I adopted on that fateful day has become my personal credo for life: I broke my neck, it didn't break me..." In his book *Man's Search for Meaning* Frankl refers to choosing one's attitude as being man's last freedom. Jerry Long chose a positive attitude.[2]

SUMMING UP

Attitude is so important. It determines almost everything in our lives. It can make relationships or it can kill them. It can cause pleasantness all around or the opposite. It can hurt others and we can hurt ourselves by it. Attitude might seem an insignificant aspect of our lives but it is powerful in its accomplishments. Through our attitude, we hold the key to achieving a positive response in others and good results for ourselves. With a wrong attitude, we can do untold damage, but with the right attitude there is no limit to the lives we might touch and change for the better. Our attitude is dictated by our thinking, by our mindset. A healthy mindset is crucial if we want to live with a right attitude which is beneficial and appreciated by those around us.

CHAPTER 6

Forgiveness Is a Tough Call

One evening Chris Williams was taking his family out to enjoy some ice cream when their car collided head-on with a vehicle driven by an under-age drunk driver. Chris lost his pregnant wife and three of his four children. Yet, strangely, even at the scene of the accident while waiting to be rescued, Chris sensed that, ultimately, he would have to forgive the other driver. Eventually, given time, he managed to achieve that, and went on to share his story for the encouragement of many others in similar situations. He is quoted as saying, "Forgive, because if you don't, your bitterness will consume you."[1]

Julie Bouvier was stabbed several times in an unprovoked attack in a shopping mall. She eventually learned that her attacker, Sean Clifton, was suffering from schizophrenia and realized that the stabbing was not against her personally. Her understanding of his situation brought her to the place of compassion and forgiveness for his actions.

Having learned personally of scenarios that have caused intolerable pain, I fully understand and appreciate the devastating sense of isolation and abandonment created by unjust and senseless hurt. If you are suffering right now in that way, I want to assure you that many of us have been in that place and share your experience. Right from our childhood days we are all aware that "I am sorry" is one of the hardest things to say. Whether we are wanting to hear those words or we are called upon to say them, they do not come easily. How many situations continue to hurt because those three small words are missing?

How sad it is when you ask someone the question, "How is your brother?" and you hear this response. "How is my brother? I wouldn't know. We haven't spoken for nine or ten years. We had a disagreement—in fact, I can't even remember what it was about now—I guess we both were proud and just drifted apart. I am not sure I even know where he lives now." That's tragic, as it is when you hear that brothers, sisters, and parents are separated, their relationships broken, all carrying possible resentment and bitterness. This is not how it was meant to be.

Forgiveness has one of the most powerful effects upon our human psyche, both from the giving and receiving of it. To give it is to be released from a prison of anger and resentment. To receive it is to be released from underlying animosity and guilt for being the cause of the rift.

Giving and receiving forgiveness are two sides of the same coin. A lack of forgiveness brings with it untold stress, which in turn causes innumerable adverse medical conditions. Research studies have shown that over 80% of illnesses are mind related. Our mental activity has an enormous direct relation to the physical. Researchers have discovered that high blood pressure, heart attacks, anxiety, depression, stomach problems, headaches, and sleeplessness can all be birthed in unforgiveness, and the resentment and bitterness that it causes. A lack of forgiveness is known to cause mental illness. In fact, I have discovered a number of scholarly works linking mental health and the need for forgiveness. Guilt takes its toll.

One of the best books I have read on the subject is *None of these Diseases*, by Dr. S. I. McMillen.[2] He so ably relates the link between the mind and the body. He outlines how it is that different parts of the anatomy are affected by different forms of mental stress, such as anxiety and guilt. The colon seems to be the favourite for reacting to stress and worry. Guilt increases the heart rate and blood pressure, both of which have an adverse effect upon the cardiovascular system.

Fortunately, forgiveness has the opposite effect and can even reverse the unwanted medical symptoms. By withholding forgiveness one does more damage to oneself than the person who is waiting for forgiveness. The person who has caused the hurt can do no more than ask for forgiveness, and then move on with life, while the other person continues to hang on to the hurt and allow it to grow larger in the mind than the original occurrence, resulting in resentment and a distasteful feeling against the adversary, which they have now become. How do these things happen?

Inevitably, we see a situation differently from someone else. We are reluctant to compromise by moving away from our position. The other person does the same, so rather than agreeing to differ and keeping the peace, we hold our ground because we firmly believe we are right. Sometimes harsh words are spoken, which results in damaging a good relationship. Both parties leave sad, disillusioned, and nursing a hurt that only forgiveness from both sides will heal. Unfortunately, this unresolved situation can continue for months and even years. The only resolution is to understand what is most important, your position or your relationship. Then consciously let go of negative emotions and maybe pride surrounding the issue, offer the "olive branch" of forgiveness, which leads to reconciliation and a repaired relationship.

We all fail at times. We all make mistakes. We let each other down. We make promises that remain unkept. We disappoint and often fall short of what was expected of us. In so doing we find ourselves standing in need of forgiveness. Remember the words we were taught to pray, "Forgive us our trespasses as we forgive those who trespass against us." Sometimes pride causes us to be reluctant to forgive. We resist apologizing because we think we are better than the one who has hurt us. Pride makes us think we must defend our ill-advised actions or our victimhood. Can we really expect forgiveness if we are unwilling to grant others forgiveness? It takes two to repair and rebuild a relationship. The good thing is that the new relationship is often stronger after the act of forgiveness, even if the healing takes time.

Although the decision to forgive comes from the mind, true forgiveness comes from the heart. I believe it originates from a compassionate heart. Compassion and forgiveness are closely linked. It is extremely difficult to have compassion and not offer forgiveness. It is said that we can only forgive to the depth of our love.

How do we forgive? How do we deal with the tremendous emotional hurt and pain when we suffer from the actions of another, whether deliberate or inadvertent? How do we overcome the enormous weight upon us that occurs when our trust in someone is destroyed? The sense of rejection is devastating. We face it. We recognize it for what it is, a hurtful barb in our own side. We recognize the suffering it is causing us but we consciously make the decision to forgive. We choose to forgive. It is an act of the will. Forgiving is definitely not an act of accepting, excusing, or condoning the behaviour that caused the hurt. It is an act of self-preservation. You choose to let go of the hurt in order to release yourself from further suffering.

Stories of forgiveness abound, and it is amazing the level of forgiveness that some people offer. There are circumstances where forgiveness could seemingly never be given, yet it is. Jake was mercilessly bullied for years. His high school life was virtually intolerable. His life was miserable. The effects stayed with him long after he graduated. He eventually came to see that those who did the bullying were no longer around but were still causing him to suffer emotionally. So he made the conscious decision to forgive his tormentors. By doing so, he found incredible release and a new life. He said it was like being released from prison.

Sarah's situation was similar to Jake's, except that she was victim of rape. She went through years of self-blame, hating herself, and thinking less and less of herself until she too recognized that her assailant, who was long gone, was still holding her hostage to the attack. She knew forgiveness was difficult but it was the only way out. Ultimately, she found it in herself to forgive, even if she could not forget, and the result was relief. The emotional weight was gone, and she too felt the wonder of release. Both Jake and Sarah indicated that their faith and trust in God gave them the strength and courage to forgive.[3]

I think also of the reaction from the Amish community when one of their local villagers shot 10 of their children and then took his own life. Incredibly, the group collectively forgave the shooter. They all attended the killer's funeral. The parents of two of the ten children killed were the first to greet the shooter's parents at his funeral. Such forgiveness is overwhelming. Forgiveness is the only way to rid the past of its dark and depressive hold over the present, even when it comes to a community.

One of the most outstanding stories of forgiveness happened almost thirty years ago. In 1992 Amy Biehl was brutally murdered by four young black men in South Africa.[4] She had gone there from her home in California on a scholarship to work with the anti-apartheid movement. A young black boy had been killed by police and tensions were running high. Amy was seen as representative of the white opposition, and in spite of protestations from black friends, she was stabbed and stoned to death. Amy believed strongly in changing people's lives by changing their circumstances. She believed economic changes would help rid the townships of poverty and squalor. This was the end to which she was working—to befriend, to help, and to change lives.

Her parents, Linda and Peter Biehl, were devastated in losing their daughter, but they were motivated and inspired to derive something positive from her sacrifice by reading Amy's diaries. They established a foundation in her name to continue her work. Thousands of dollars were donated. Linda and Peter went to South Africa to see the places their daughter had been and to meet the people with whom she had been working. Using Peter's business experience, they organized development projects there for the benefit of the locals. People were trained and employed in welding, sewing, printing, and in a bakery. They founded a construction company, built sports facilities, and introduced adult literacy programs.

The most amazing and incredible aspect of their story occurred when they met two of their daughter's killers. Bishop Desmond Tutu had established a Truth and Reconciliation Commission, which provided the opportunity for reconciliation between the opposing sides of apartheid, and attempted to turn hatred into love. The

Biehls wanted to be part of that by offering forgiveness to Amy's killers. It was not easy. Real forgiveness is never easy, it takes choice, willpower, and determination.

To their utter surprise, two of these men, Easy Nofomela and Ntobeko Peni, turned up at their foundation after being released from prison. They wanted to help. The foundation hired them. Linda and Peter Biehl recognized what courage it took for these men to come to their door and they admired them for it. An amazing relationship has been built between them over many years of working together. Ntobeko stated, "I don't know how they found it in their hearts to forgive us, but I can tell you it has greatly enriched my life. I will never forget the kindness they have shown me when they had every reason to hate me."

When asked about it, Linda Biehl says "Forgiveness is really about liberating yourself, letting go, so you can be rid of hate and bitterness. It's a one-way street that doesn't need the other person to do anything . . . Reconciliation is a different step. It's really hard work." Talking about their Christian faith, Linda says, "It's one of the things that was important to us, that we not be hypocritical; it was important that we don't say one thing and do something else. It was important to try to do what we believe and act out in a positive way." They certainly did that, and in doing so they changed the lives of many people for the better.

I think of Nelson Mandela, who was held for 27 years as a political prisoner. He forgave those who put him there. He said that hatred and bitterness are destructive—power is in love and forgiveness. He is reported to have said "Resentment is like drinking poison and then hoping it will kill your enemies." While we hold on to the anger, resentment, and bitterness created by the pain we suffer from the action of others, we allow them to continue to hurt us. Once we choose to let go and forgive, it is we who are released from a self-imposed prison. We are those who gain the freedom, peace, and serenity. The weight is lifted. We feel free. Why would we ever hang on to our anger and resentment when we know it will do ourselves a great emotional and physical disservice? Unfortunately, we do.

James E. Faust, an American religious leader, lawyer, and politician once said, "If we can find forgiveness in our hearts for those who have caused us hurt and injury, we will rise to a higher level of self-esteem and well-being." Forgiveness does not change the past but it certainly makes a difference to the future.

When I look at the times in my life when I experienced hurts which led to forgiveness, they pale into insignificance when I think about the atrocities that have occurred against others. Yet these people have found it in their hearts to forgive. When we consider parents forgiving those who have murdered their child, we find it astounding and difficult to understand. That is an extraordinary act of forgiveness. We wonder how that could be done. It can only be through the incredible power of love.

Mother Teresa once said, "If we really want to love, we must learn to forgive." Who benefits from such a sacrificial act of love? It is always those who let go of the hurt. They are released from their incessant pain. We should not allow the act of giving or receiving forgiveness rob us of our peace of mind. When Jesus was asked whether we should forgive seven times, his reply was "Seventy times seven," which indicated not a specific number, but that we should forgive endlessly. He emphasized that we should be liberal with our forgiveness that we in turn may receive forgiveness.

FORGIVING OURSELVES

Margaret was twenty-seven and had two small children. She was on her way to visit her mother just a few miles from home. Driving her car with the two children happily strapped in their car seats, Margaret was nonchalantly following behind a small pick-up truck on a two-lane road. Suddenly the truck hit a bump, the tailgate opened and a large wooden box fell to the ground right in front of her. She braked and swerved at the same time. She hit the heavy box with the right front of her car but the back of her car swung out into the path of an oncoming vehicle.

Unfortunately, the other driver lost control and crashed the car. He was quite seriously hurt. Tragically, Margaret found herself in the middle of a nightmare. Although the airbags had inflated, her chest was hurting. The children were screaming in the back seat. Soon the police and ambulance arrived. She sensed that an officer was talking to her. The paramedics were there also asking questions. Fortunately, she and the children were not suffering with any serious injury, but in the haze of the moment she felt her world had suddenly fallen apart.

In Margaret's mind everything was a mess. "How could this happen," she thought. They were now faced with a big car repair bill and she was told she may face a charge of entering the other lane and causing an accident. What would she tell her husband? If only she had left more space between her car and the vehicle ahead. If only she had left earlier or later. The more she thought about the situation, the worse she felt about it and herself. She tortured herself with thoughts of how different things might have been. The negative "if only" thoughts kept coming. However, she worried needlessly. Her husband understood completely and was glad his family were safe. The charge did not materialize, as the accident was not her fault. But the whole episode left Margaret shaken, very disturbed, and in pretty low spirits. She could not stop thinking that somehow it was her fault. It took several months, but eventually she forgave herself and recovered, but not without a visit to a counsellor.

Occasionally we find it difficult to forgive ourselves. As humans we make mistakes, sometimes with devastating results. How many times have we wished to go back in time and undo the things we may have done or said, thoughtlessly or carelessly? Time has passed and we still feel a sense of guilt about it. People may have even moved away or passed on and we wish we had the opportunity again to say "sorry," but it is no longer available. It continues to bother us mentally. How do we deal with that? We can still genuinely offer them forgiveness from our heart so we clear it from our mind. Sometimes it helps to write it out on paper so that we make it a tangible and practical act. We can then be free to forgive ourselves and move on with life.

SUMMING UP

Only you know if your situation is calling for an act of forgiveness. Maybe there is something stored in the recesses of your mind that you know should be sorted out. You have tried to bury it, yet you find it still keeps rising to the surface and continues to bother you. You know deep down that forgiveness is necessary to resolve the issue. However difficult, for the sake of our health, we have to learn to forgive or receive forgiveness. To heal that broken friendship, that fractured relationship, takes just one person to act humbly and make the move towards resolution. Hard? Yes, but the end result is worth it. "I'm sorry" is hard to say but the freedom it brings is unsurpassed. The American author, H. Jackson Brown, Jr, said, "Never forget the three powerful resources you always have available to you, love, prayer and forgiveness." Forgiveness is not a sign of weakness or giving in, it is a sign of strength. It takes strength and determination to forgive and to move on. Forgiven! What a wonderful word? But even better is the experience.

CHAPTER 7

Why Do We Crave Significance?

Jane was approaching mid-life. Once her children were well entrenched in high school she decided to go back to work. After seventeen years faithfully working in the office of a manufacturer, she came face to face with the dreaded pink slip. It was completely unexpected. The surprise shocked and disturbed her immensely. She was told it was due to a company reorganization and consolidation. Two others were let go at the same time, but for Jane it was a devastating experience. Immediately she began to question herself. Had she been incompetent in her work? Was she not able to keep up with the flow of work? Was she not accepting of the new changes and the more modern approach to the work? She thought the company had considered her a valued worker. Her thoughts rotated endlessly. She could not get away from blaming herself. Because of that and her feeling of shame, she found it difficult to explain her layoff to family and friends. Unfortunately, as she allowed her blame to grow, her self-worth deteriorated. In fact, it ultimately led to a depression. I believe Jane is not alone in her self-incrimination. Many others would do the same and can identify with her thinking. This kind of situation is so unfortunate because Jane did not need to blame herself, but regrettably she did.

How quickly life can become a blame game, even against ourselves. It does not take much to think less of ourselves. One mistake, one adverse situation, and our sense of self-worth begins to decline. Our self-esteem quickly dissipates. We immediately think, "What will others think of me?" and "Where did I go wrong?" Our sense of significance is diminished as we come down heavy on ourselves. In a world where significance is equated with performing well, being successful and attaining a high level of achievement, it is not surprising that many of us feel inadequate, especially when things go wrong and we think we have failed. We assume we no longer measure up to the expected standard of significance.

Twice in life we are all equal. At birth we arrive with nothing, and at death we take nothing with us. We leave everything behind. Billionaire or pauper, president or peasant, we are all equal when it comes to birth and death. You must have heard the proverbial question asked of a wealthy man, "How much did he leave?" "Everything," is the answer. What we possess has nothing to do with our significance.

The common understanding of significance in the twenty-first century is to be recognized for having wealth, power, and possessions. Our society generally believes that holding a prominent position, having money in the bank, owning property, owning exotic cars, and pursuing a luxurious life style, creates significance. The motivational gurus of our day put forth their message that you can "have it all" with the mantra that, "If you can think it, you can achieve it!" Consequently people spend billions of dollars in seeking that illusive "have it all" result. They attend lectures and conventions. They buy courses that supposedly hold the secret to incredible wealth, only to find that the wealth has gone to those offering the secrets. Perhaps a little generalization on my part, but it holds a huge element of truth.

Wealthy people are revered. Some have used their wealth to set up charitable trusts and made substantial contributions to the less fortunate. Their philanthropic activity is admirable and commendable. Yet it is because of their wealth they are held in high esteem. Their possessions are equated with significance and success. Yet some of their biographies tell another story. They discovered their money was not enough to bring personal satisfaction and significance. Some sadly committed suicide because they sensed their lives were meaningless, even in the midst of their wealth. We have seen a similar tragedy with celebrities who have taken their own lives. It was not because they were poor or not held in high esteem. In spite of what they had in life, they lost their sense of significance and self-esteem.

WHY AM I HERE?

Deep down, we humans have an insatiable desire to find meaning and purpose for our existence. Inwardly we are driven by this quest. Some people call it a search for significance. Significance is inevitably tied to the question of "Who am I?" Significance is important to all of us. Very few of us do not yearn for it deep down. We all desire a life full of meaning and purpose. It may be just a desire to be personally recognized by others; or perhaps we want to achieve something significant in our lifetime. None of us wants to be just a meaningless speck floating on the ocean of life, or just a blip on the universal radar screen. We want to know that, ultimately, we have made a difference for our being here. We would like to know that the world is a better place because of our presence. Many of us desire to leave our mark after we have gone, that ultimately, we have written our name on the wall to say, "I was here." These are often the factors that motivate and drive us in our search for meaning and significance.

Robert S. McGee, in his book *Search for Significance* says, "Whether labeled *self-esteem* or *selfworth*, the feeling of significance is crucial to man's emotional, spiritual, and social stability and is the driving element within the human spirit. Understanding this single need opens the door to understanding our actions and attitudes."[1]

None of us wants to feel insignificant. We all need a sense of well-being, a reason for being. We need a sense of purpose, of meaning and acceptance. We desire to have a sense of importance. We want to feel we are needed. We want to make a difference. These aspects are all wrapped up in significance. Can we live without it? Probably, but it would not be pleasant, and in fact could be quite depressing. Feeling insignificant is painful and it is not something that we like to openly acknowledge.

I am certain there are times when we all face such questions as, "Why am I here?" or "What is my purpose in life?" Some people call these the big questions of life, and seeking answers to them becomes a spiritual quest. For centuries philosophers have attempted to answer these big questions as they relate to humankind, with little success. Some readily admit that life appears to be pointless, having little purpose except to be born, procreate, and die. Some consider that we are just a cosmic accident. Our discussion here, however, relates to our personal meaning and significance.

I remember a friend talking to me about job satisfaction. He had held some important leadership roles in the corporate world but he displayed a sense of frustration about his life. He indicated that in spite of all his success—the position, the cars, the houses he possessed—he would readily change places with me, for, he considered the fact that the mission work I had been involved with in Eastern Europe held far more purpose and satisfaction than anything he had ever achieved. He was seeking an answer to the meaning and purpose of his life. He was beginning to wonder what kind of a mark he would leave behind.

You are not alone if other people have damaged or minimized your sense of significance. It is quite common for negative statements made about us to cause a low sense of significance. Sadly, we do allow the words of others to influence our thinking about ourselves. As we have already said earlier, we are prone to highlight the negative and downplay the compliments. But our significance, or self-worth, is not based upon the approval of others. The view that others hold of us can be, and very often is, based on false information. False accusations hurt immensely. I know from experience. There was a time I was publicly accused of embezzlement, which was not only untrue but impossible, as I did not have signing authority or handle the finances of the organization in question. Fortunately, I had the presence of mind to allow the truth to rise to the surface. It was later discovered that the accuser had a personal vendetta against someone in our family. The whole experience was anything but pleasant and certainly hit hard at my self-esteem, as the accusation was made publicly. You may have experienced something similar—accusations made, unfounded in truth and reality. Maybe only you know the truth.

WHERE DO WE FIND REAL MEANING?

Although how you view yourself is critical to your self-worth, what is more important is how God views us, and I believe therein lies the secret of our significance. To find real meaning, purpose, and significance, we are forced to look beyond the bounds of our own limited mind. We need to look outside the confinement of our own life. I believe the answer is spiritual. From what I have seen, read, and have come to understand, God is an integral part of life's equation. Without God, I believe, life becomes meaningless. Without God, life does not make sense. For me, life without God is a puzzle. I believe it is only in God that we will find the answers that satisfy. God created humanity for himself, so that all of life pertains to God. Without this understanding, it is difficult to make sense of life and its purpose.

Our significance is not then derived from what we own or what we have achieved. It is not the accomplished feeling from a position of power or authority. It is not indicated by our abilities, our profession, or our achievements. It is determined by who we are. It comes from recognizing the importance of who we are. That importance—our significance and self-worth—is based upon the approval of God and not the approval of society or others around us. If we base our significance on the acceptance and approval of those around us. I think we will be sadly disappointed. We have a choice, listen to our mind—which can easily lead us astray in our thinking—or listen to our heart. Our heart knows the truth. Our heart will confirm our significance. It will assure us that we have no reason to put ourselves down. We are valued and worthy. We have significance.

When people make a valuable contribution to society, in whatever form it takes, they are considered significant, and rightly so. However, that is totally different and unrelated to our personal significance. Our personal significance is based upon our value as a human being. Psychologist Lawrence Crabb Jr. said, "The basic personal need of each person is to regard himself as a worthwhile human being." Our significance is based upon our value and we are all of equal value in this life. It matters not what power or position we hold. Consequently, we have no need to prove anything to anyone; we are a worthy human being in our own right.

As we saw earlier with Jane, when life caves in on us and we feel overwhelmed, we often start blaming ourselves. We begin to think less of ourselves and wonder what is wrong with us. Because significance goes hand in hand with self-worth and self-esteem, our significance takes a hit when we start thinking that way. We need to look beyond what happens to us or around us. We need to ignore what others have said or inferred about us, because none of that changes our significance. We are significant because God made us and nothing will change that.

We will always be significant in his eyes. I like what Max Lucado says, "You weren't an accident. You weren't mass produced. You aren't an assembly line product. You were deliberately planned, specifically gifted, and lovingly positioned on the earth by the Master Craftsman."

SUMMING UP

If you have been suffering with low self-esteem and a loss of significance in your life, then take heart. Your significance is well and truly in place. Just believe it and accept it. You may think you can't believe that but it makes no difference to the truth. When people thought the earth was flat, it made no difference to the fact that it was round. Whether you believe it or not makes no difference to the truth that God made you, and to him you will always be significant. You need to hear it, believe it, embrace it, and delight yourself in the fact that your significance is real. You are important. You are invaluable to those around you. You are special and nothing can change that. Accept it and be encouraged. Move forward confidently, knowing that your significance is intact and no one can remove that from you. You are who you are, and you are loved and accepted for who you are. Revel in that thought.

CHAPTER 8

It's Okay to be Ordinary

It's more than okay to be ordinary. It's more than okay to be normal. As humans, we respond to certain circumstances with emotion. We respond with laughter and joy to the humorous and the celebratory occasion. We respond with anger and sadness to things that upset us and cause us disappointment. We are brought to tears by what hurts. But it is all right to cry. Crying is the emotional safety valve given to us to rid ourselves of pent-up inner feelings of turmoil and frustration. People cry themselves to sleep night after night when going through a tough period of life, perhaps feeling an acute loneliness or being faced with an insoluble situation. Crying is therapeutic. It brings emotional release and calms our disposition, from which we can then evaluate our situation. It's okay to cry.

Whether from books or the Internet, we are constantly bombarded with challenges to reach our full potential.

For some of us, these are unrealistic expectations because many of us do not have what it takes to be a superstar. And there's nothing wrong with that, because being ourselves is very acceptable. Who knows? Perhaps we have already reached our potential. We may be happy in the place we find ourselves or at the point we have reached in life. These encouragements for us to gain success can easily make us feel inadequate with our present life. They infer that we are missing out big-time, because someone else suggests we have not achieved our maximum potential in life. It can make us feel dissatisfied with what we may have already achieved in life. Perhaps we need to ignore those inferences. Our full potential differs with each of us and only we know how satisfied we are with our life as it is.

Thousands of people reach fulfilment in life without being at the top of the company sales chart, without sitting in the big chair in the corporate office, or receiving public accolades for being the outstanding citizen of the month. Many people reach their full potential by simply caring and providing for their family, by encouraging their children, being an appreciative wife or husband, or by caring for an incapacitated child, parent, or spouse. These may not be outstanding accomplishments if compared to financial achievements, but that is not the only measure of success or fulfillment.

Success is the result of achieving whatever you set out to do. You have a goal. You have a purpose you want to fulfil. It could be anything. It may have nothing to do with attaining financial freedom. It may have nothing to do with a professional career. It may be just setting yourself a simple target of writing a daily journal entry. It could be going to the gym or getting out to walk regularly. It could be deliberately spending more time with your spouse or children one-on-one. It may be building a tree-house or playhouse for your kids. Or it could be something bigger on your wish list, like climbing a mountain or visiting abroad. Anything you set out to do and ultimately achieve it, is success.

If you are like most of us, normal, ordinary people, you're fine. That is how we are and we have no reason to think any less of ourselves. We may not align ourselves with those who indicate that life is a failure until one gains status and recognition in the public arena, but that's all right. Our importance and worthiness as a human being is not predicated on any measurement of success. You are not odd if you have no desire to be a superstar.

If you are married, you have probably said to your spouse or had it said to you, "I just want you to be happy." Parents have said the same to their children. Well, who doesn't want to be happy? Not only do people want to be happy but they want others around them to be happy, especially within the family. Research shows that happy people live 7 to 10 years longer than average. I also found a publicized list of 215 books with titles on achieving happiness or closely related topics. Obviously, the desire for happiness—and the pursuit of it—ranks high on many people's agenda.

Well, what is happiness? Is it having a sense of fulfillment? Is it the result of a personal achievement? Is it contentment? Is happiness knowing that all is well and everything is ticking along nicely in your world? Is it just the absence of problems, obstacles, disagreements, or not having to face personal illness or tragedy? Happiness comes partially from our surrounding circumstances, but ongoing happiness comes from within. Happiness from circumstances fluctuates as situations change. Real happiness comes from our inward state. A dictionary definition suggests it is the pleasure derived from contentment. I believe that's the crucial word—contentment! Perhaps, then, contentment should be our primary focus, and happiness will follow. How then can we experience contentment? The answer to that could be different for each of us.

ARE YOU CONTENTED?

So, are you contented? Are you satisfied with your life as it is right now? Maybe you are, and that's good. Not everyone is in a state of dissatisfaction and feeling as though the world has fallen in. But perhaps you are unhappy. Your situation right now may be the cause of anything but happiness. Perhaps you long to see things change. You wish certain people would act differently. You feel your circumstances have you hemmed in on every side. Happiness and contentment seem to be elusive but you would love that to change. If that is so, then perhaps it is time for you to stop, check, revise, and maybe redirect your focus.

When I was in my mid-twenties I had this idea that I wanted to write a book. I tried, but it did not fly. However, I did write freelance articles and reviews for years after that.

The idea of a book was always there but life happened and time passed. I made another attempt when in my fifties, but I listened to a colleague who offered nothing but negative comments about the project. He put water on the fire and it went out. Twelve years later, after I had retired, I read about a man who wrote five books between his seventy fifth and ninetieth birthday. Reading that caused me to resurrect my previous ambition to write a book. It took me two years, one year to research and one year to write. By the time I was seventy I had published my first book. Now eleven years later, this is my fourth. I would like to call that success, satisfaction, and contentment all wrapped in one package.

Contentment comes from being occupied with a task you enjoy. It means being involved in something meaningful each day. Normally contentment comes from being excited about what you are doing and having purpose in it. It allows you to experience a real sense of freedom in your mind and spirit. Perhaps this is not your situation at the moment and you wish it were. There is nothing wrong with desiring something better. You don't have to be totally dissatisfied with your circumstance before you seek to improve your situation. In fact, a healthy, mentally balanced position is where one strives for better things while being satisfied with the present.

I mentioned earlier that we are told we should be living life to the full but what does that mean. I guess it means a life that resonates with enthusiasm and carries some excitement with it, a life that is not boring. A life where we are eager to get up in the morning because we know we have a purpose for the day. Some days we know a special event is to take place and we get up with keenness and expectation of enjoying the day. Why shouldn't each of our days be like that? I find it really sad when a person says that his or her life is boring. They are obviously missing so much from life and very definitely life for them could be better. No one lives at the top of their performance day after day. Nobody lives on top of the mountain every day. We all have valleys through which we trudge, some of which are dark and bothersome and some seem to go on forever. Maybe you are in one of those valleys right now. It's at those times we wish for better things, better circumstances. We wish life would change. We long for life to improve.

Regrettably some people raise their own mental hurdles. I have heard it said, "I am what I am and that's how I am. I have always been like this and don't see any changes coming soon. I know it sounds pretty hopeless but I don't seem to have the ability to change." If you have any thoughts that way I would urge you not to believe that lie. We all have what it takes to change, and change for the better. When we listen to our hearts we instinctively know what we have to do. Our heart somehow knows the truth. We know we have to fix what needs fixing and that normally implements a change. It will call for strength and courage. It will call for determination and motivation, because change is rarely easy.

Sometimes the predicaments and difficulties we find ourselves in obscure the way forward, and we find it difficult to determine exactly where we want to go and what changes we want to see. Sickness, financial struggles, broken relationships, or other forms of life's obstacles may have left you with an inability to see the way forward. The blocks in the road ahead are too big for you to see around. You long for the blocks to be removed. Once they are removed you know the road ahead will be clearer. Maybe you will need to seek help from outside to get the obstacles removed—a counsellor or trusted friend. At times we need help to see further than our immediate problems. An objective viewpoint can be enlightening and helpful. Maybe the only change you would like to see at the moment is the removal of your financial burden, your physical sickness, or the repairing of a broken relationship. If that is so, then work toward that end.

But others can go further by asking such questions as, "Are there changes I can make for the better," or, "Am I making the most of my life?" or, "Is there a different road I can take that would improve my circumstances?" Most of us readily know the answers. The sad thing is that we often just drift along from situation to situation, going with the flow wherever it takes us, not really seizing control and giving direction to our journey. Perhaps it is time to ensure we have control of the rudder and begin to steer the boat in the right direction. To do so may call for a change, perhaps a radical change. Things that matter do not happen by chance but by choice. Life does not get better by chance but by making the decision to change.

ACCEPTING THE INEVITABLE

Few people welcome change. C. S. Lewis, in *The Screwtape Letters*, said, "To be in time means to change." We are told that the only constant thing in life is change. Everything changes around us, and we do too. We change in appearance and we change mentally, hopefully for the better. Changes are often difficult to accept. A man who had attended one church for forty-six years was asked if he had seen many changes in that time. His reply was, "I have seen many changes here and have opposed them all!" We cannot stop change in the world around us. We have to face it and accept it. We may have to do the same in our personal life. To embrace it is the best way forward.

It may mean accepting a new phase of life, maybe a new location, meeting new people, doing different things, changing daily activity and programs, giving up routine habits, stepping outside our comfort zone. That is the way to grow mentally and emotionally. Until we break free we will never know what might be out there for us and what we might achieve. It is not easy to step outside our self-imposed circle, but once we do it brings an overwhelming freedom. Leo Tolstoy said, "Everyone thinks of changing the world, but no one thinks of changing himself."

To make changes for the better requires having the intent and then the determination to act. Obviously, it all starts with thinking, but then we need to look at the practical issues of change—ones that will improve our situation—and do what we can do to implement them.

We need to see beyond today. We need to visualize the big picture, perhaps a better life, a better job, changed relationships, a changed life.

Change for the better does not happen overnight. It all starts with a minute shift. A small, almost imperceptible change in direction creates big changes further down the road. Just as a minuscule degree change in trajectory when launching a space craft can cause it to miss the target by millions of miles, a small change in your habits, outlook, discipline, and action can bring huge results later. If you are looking for changes in your life, then start small. Trying to change too much or implement huge changes at once only brings discouragement. Make the easy changes first. Don't rush. Give yourself time to implement a new regimen. A simple example is if you are looking to get up an hour earlier to give you more time for a new habit, then set your clock ten minutes earlier each day for six days. We are told that if we do something new daily for a month it sets us on the road to creating a habit. We shape our own pathway by the effort expended.

Most of us stay within our comfort zone until circumstances push us out. We feel secure where we are. Comfort zones are the places where we feel comfortable and safe. If, however, we want to go to new places in our lives or achieve something we aspire to, then it will call for us to expand that comfort zone, to stretch ourselves. Ronald Osborn, an American teacher and writer, said, "Unless you try to do something beyond what you have already mastered, you will never grow." We all want to be the best we can and use what we have to that end. Don't be afraid to look over the fence and see where you have never been. Who knows, maybe the grass is greener over the fence. Once we arrive at the new place we will wonder why we were so tentative and cautious. Once there, we are glad we made the effort. We discover that what we thought impossible became possible before our eyes. Things are impossible only if we allow them to be.

We all change over time, not just physically but in our understanding and in our thinking. Whether it is progression or just changing lanes, new thoughts and ideas come into play and stimulate our thinking. We change positions. We reposition ourselves according to our new thinking. If we never change, then we are not thinking. Change is inevitable. This is where we need to accept it, go with the flow, and use it to our own advantage. If we were sailing it would mean setting the sails according to the wind. If we want to get "there" then we need to move ourselves away from "here." Only we can do that. We have to adopt change if we want to progress and grow. To build a house, build a road, in fact, to build anything requires change. All new projects begin with change. Get the first change in motion and others will follow.

In looking at who we are today, we might think it just happened without any planning. That is not so. In fact, we have developed and been shaped by a myriad of influences, both good and bad. People we live with, work with, study with, or associate with all played a vital part in who we have become, whether we like to think so or not. Circumstances and events in our lives also added their part, both positive and negative. We have probably been changed by success and influenced by failure. Hopefully, we gained insight and learned from both. We needed a right attitude and a positive mindset in order to do that.

So we ask ourselves, "Are we happy with who we have become?" For instance, if you had the opportunity to meet yourself, what would your reaction be? Would you be pleased to meet yourself? We are not talking about personality but the person we are socially and internally. Perhaps we see areas where we would like to be different. Perhaps we need to have more understanding, be more compassionate, or maybe have a more caring attitude.

SUMMING UP

We know in ourselves there is always room for improvement, for learning, and for changing. Even if difficult, attempt to make those changes you know will be for the better—better for yourself and others. Recognize the benefits that will come from the change and take action. Be bold. Be strong, for your own sake and those around you. You may need to ask God for wisdom and strength to make changes that count. It certainly will take determination and effort, but go ahead, you can do it, make the necessary changes and be more comfortable with who you are. You need to be happy with who you have become or who you are becoming. I know you can be. Think it through, bring the beneficial changes into effect and it will reward you with a real sense of contentment. Happiness will follow.

CHAPTER 9

Touch a Person — Change a Life

Some people are more than amazing. Their lives are simply outstanding. Their achievements are mind-blowing. Such a person is Nick Vujicic. His story is told in the book *Life without Limits*.[1] Nick was born without limbs. Think about that for a moment— no arms and no legs—and what that might mean. Even the shocked parents found it hard initially to accept the situation, but they cared for him deeply and insisted people treat him as normal as possible. They sent him to public school. Obviously, it is an understatement to say his life was hard in so many ways. He really was helpless and had to rely constantly upon others for virtually everything.

As he grew older he suffered periods of depression and wanted to end his life, but miraculously, he gradually overcame such desires and thinking. He began talking openly about his life and struggles, first to fellow student groups and then to church groups. He shared how he overcame his disadvantages, and people warmed to his story. Astonishing as it may sound, and in spite of his mobility challenges, Nick was drawn to the idea of being a public speaker. By grit and determination he eventually and incredibly became just that, a public speaker, addressing thousands in many countries, sharing a message of hope and encouragement.

Nick's story changed many lives. Generally, the public's response was, "If he can achieve what he has achieved with such disadvantages and be as happy as he is with such a handicap, then surely I can do the same, having far fewer obstacles to overcome." People were changed, challenged, and uplifted in their spirit. His expressed desire was to make other people's lives better. This he did, time and time again. People would respond to him after meetings, or upon seeing his videos on YouTube, with the words, "You changed my life." This was Nick's goal and he succeeded in achieving just that.

I don't believe that we can change people at will, but I do believe we have the ability to influence people for the better. People do respond to a positive and encouraging attitude. Dale Partridge, a well-known online pastor, has said, "You were born with the ability to change someone's life; don't waste it!" If that is true, we need to be looking to seize opportunities to do just that. We need to be encouraging others so that their lives reflect a mountain-top experience. But how do we do that? How do we make someone's life better? Well, our words are important, but as you know, our actions speak louder than our words, so we have to show that we care. It is true that people don't care how much you know until they know how much you care. We have to show in tangible ways that we are there for them on bad days and good days, through thick and thin, when life is turbulent or calm.

You may be feeling however, that it is hard for you to make a difference in someone else's life while your own situation is desperately calling for a change. You may think to yourself, *I can help once I see my life improving.* Well, the ironic aspect of life is that by helping others you help yourself. If ever there were a two-sided coin in the area of self-healing, it is in serving other people. It is a fact that we are happiest when serving others. Time and again it has been proven that by serving others, doing something for someone else's benefit without looking for a return, brings its own rewards. We recognize a need and reach out to help bring a solution and find that the boomerang of joy and satisfaction comes full circle. Serving others helps to keep self-deprecation and self-pity at bay. We take our eyes off ourselves and concentrate on others. We invest in the lives of others and the dividends come back to us. It turns our attention away from our problems to see the needs of others.

Edna Harrison-Harlin was sixty years old when her husband died; she was devastated. She said, "In losing my husband, I felt like Job of old, I had lost everything." Yet while still in that state of despair she turned her attention to helping others in a similar situation. She invited those who had lost loved ones through death, separation, or divorce to a meeting in her home, which she called, "New Lease on Life." At the meeting, they would just share and pray together. The gatherings were so successful that they expanded to other cities across the United States. Unknowingly and inadvertently, Edna changed many lives for the better.[2]

She went on to write a book entitled, *A Second Chance at Love*. In it she shared the inspiration that brought her out of despair. She wrote, "God meets us at our point of weakness." She continued, "... God began to work in ways that were beyond my wildest dreams. He showed me that helping others would also help me. It is a strange but proven biblical principle, 'give and you shall receive.'" Actually, the end of her story is that she did receive something in return. Out of her new connections she found a new husband, hence the title of her book.

What can we offer to make a difference? How do we reach out and touch the lives of others? If we have the desire, invariably the opportunity will present itself. Without looking for it, a gap will appear that we know we can fill. As we become sensitive to the needs of others, doors of service will open. As humans, we are interdependent. If we truly understand that, we will want to support and lift up those who are down. We are told that the greatest commandment is to love God with all our heart, soul, and strength, but the second commandment is to love our neighbour as ourselves which, if we think about it, is quite the task. True love for others will express itself in compassion, kindness, and forgiveness. Concern for others will replace self-absorption. What a wonderful world it would be if we put others first! Love would replace hate. Courtesy would replace selfish action. Unfortunately, that is not the world we live in.

Our society is primarily self-centered. This partially is natural, as life revolves around us as we care for ourselves and families. Looking beyond that however, we see in our society a deep craving for a life of luxury. Unfortunately, when that becomes all consuming, the needs of others are quickly overlooked and disappear. There is nothing wrong with being ambitious and wanting to provide adequately for your family, but if in doing so others are exploited, ignored, or even trodden upon, then something is wrong. I understand that if we have a bank account and have money in our pocket, we are among the world's richest 10%. If we are in that group I guess we carry some responsibility to reach out and help.

So then, how do we show our concern? How do we make a difference in our world? We can start anywhere. Consider those you associate with on a daily basis—your family, your friends, your acquaintances, people you regularly rub shoulders with in the store or at the bus stop. Most people have needs. Find out how they are faring in life. Genuinely enquire of their well-being. What support do they need? What encouragement would give them a boost? It doesn't have to be something large or outstanding. Words of encouragement run deep. Even strangers warm to positive comments and compliments. It takes only thoughtfulness to say, "Well done. You are doing a great job!" or "You are looking very smart today!" Only a few words, but the effect is long-lasting. That is all it might take to help someone feel their worth, their value, and give them a sense of being on top of the world for that day. Many people just need to know that someone cares about them and for them. Often it is the little things of life that mean so much. I read of a lady who was just given a copy of the poem, "Footprints in the Sand." It changed her life. It brought the realization that she was not alone when going through suffering and emotional turmoil.

We need each other. People need people. We might think and act independently but we are made for community. This is why we need real friendships, not just acquaintances. We need to have those around us who will be there, not only when the sun shines, but also when the rains lash down and the winds of life create havoc. Real friends stand with us in such storms. They overlook our faults, love us and stand with us anyway. They are people upon whom we can rely. We all need such support. It confirms that we are loved and accepted as we are. But friendship is a two-way street. We need to be offering that kind of friendship to others.

LOVE IS THE KEY

Love, compassion, and kindness are the way forward if we want to touch lives and make the world a better place. Our genuine love for others will show itself in compassionate acts of kindness. Loving someone is a powerful force that benefits both giver and receiver. Giving love to another creates returns and rewards that always outweigh the love expended. Others will respond in kind far beyond the love they have received. The adage, "to give is better than to receive," is proved again and again when reaching out in love to those in need. It seems that we do ourselves a favour, and are lifted up in spirit, when we are able to touch another life by sharing.

Serving others brings with it a sense of peace, purpose, and satisfaction. It helps to remove negativity, such as criticism and complaining. It produces a sense of happiness and contentment. Your small kindness or contribution to someone else's life might prove to be the exact answer or solution to their need at that moment. Mother Teresa said, "Spread love everywhere you go. Let no one ever come to you without leaving happier."

Emotional pain is impossible to measure, but pain is pain, and it hurts. Sometimes all we can offer is an arm around the shoulder. It may not seem much but it says, "I care." It says, "I'm here to support you. I am here to love you through this." It indicates a willingness to share the burden. It says "I love you. Let me share your pain."

Love—such a small word but so powerful in its effect. For centuries, it has been the subject of literature, plays, and operas. Probably the most popular subject of books and films. In a book of quotations I found almost three hundred entries on love, more than any other subject. Can you imagine a world without love? It would not make for a pleasant existence. Love is like an invisible glue that creates stability in society. We all crave to be loved and accepted. Love brings happiness, contentment, confidence, and a sense of security in the one who is loved. The outward expression of love is powerful. It comforts, it brings strength, consolidates relationships, and establishes new ones. So how do we express that love to those who need to be loved? It's all in the form of caring and kindness.

Caring for someone expresses your love for them. No words are needed. You feel what others are feeling. You put yourself into the other person's shoes. You attempt to understand the road they are travelling and the obstacles they face. It means getting into another person's head, to feel the emotional pain and suffering they are experiencing. This is compassion in action. Compassion will always find a way to express itself. In the life of Jesus, we read that he had compassion on the crowds of people, and what did he do? He fed the hungry and healed the sick, a very practical demonstration of compassion.

KINDNESS IS THE VEHICLE

Sometimes to act in kindness will call for vulnerability. It may mean stepping out of our comfort zone or doing something that is normally foreign to us. It means overcoming self-consciousness. It means momentarily forgetting ourselves. We do not automatically think of others first, therefore it takes effort deliberately to choose to respond to someone else's need. In doing so we too enjoy the repercussions. In fact, performing acts of kindness can even lower blood pressure. To give a word of encouragement costs nothing. To buy a coffee or a meal for a homeless person is very little in comparison to the result. Volunteer at the food bank or at your local senior residence. Keep company with those who get no visitors. It shows you care and that they are not alone.

Kindness is a matter of the will. Kindness means going the extra mile. J.R.R.Tolkien said, "Some believe it is only great power that can hold evil in check, but it is not what I have found. It is the small everyday deeds of ordinary folk that keep the darkness at bay by small acts of kindness and love." Kindness is being sensitive to the needs of others and then seeking to do something to meet those needs, be they physical or emotional. A small investment into kindness brings big dividends. There is a wonderful quotation by Tolstoy who said, "Nothing can make our lives, or the lives of others, more beautiful than perpetual kindness."

About 30 years ago we received a telephone call from friends in England. Friends of theirs – a mother and daughter – were in trouble. They were on a visit to Canada and apparently were being treated intolerably by the people with whom they were staying. We were asked if we could help. My wife and I drove the fifty miles to find these people, extricated them from their situation, gave them accommodation, and cared for them until it was time for them to return to England. Years later, Christmas cards still remind us of that much-appreciated event. A little kindness can produce outstanding and long lasting results.

Think about this. An eleven-year-old girl with an inoperable brain tumour sees other children with cancer in the hospital where she is receiving treatment and says, "Dad, how can we help them?" After that visit, with a heart of compassion and without any prompting, she took lunch bags, decorated them with stickers, and began filling them with toys. She had planned to give her whole collection of Beanie Babies to these children.

In the book, *Never Ever Give Up*, one can read the very moving story of this young girl, Jessica Rees, as told by her father, Erik Rees.[3] Realizing the lunch bags were inadequate for what his daughter wanted to achieve, he purchased clear plastic containers. These were filled with toys and goodies, and Jessica began distributing them to the other children in between her treatments. They called them "JoyJars" after Jessica's middle name, Joy. Soon word got out about what she was doing, and family, friends, and neighbours became involved.

What started out at the local hospital spread across the United States, and finally, to twenty-seven countries around the world. It all began from the mind of a little girl who was concerned for other children. Jessica encouraged everyone around her with the motto NEGU—Never Ever Give Up. Sadly, she succumbed to her illness ten months after her diagnosis. Jessica may be gone but thousands of children around the world suffering from cancer are benefitting because of her kindness, her loving attitude, and the willingness to ignore her own plight and concentrate on others. Considering her thinking and action, I hope and pray that regardless of our circumstances, we would have the same desire, compassion, and kindness. It is this kind of attitude and action that changes the world for the better.

CHAPTER 10

Who Is My Neighbour?

Would you help pick someone up from the street if they fell down in front of you? Not everybody would. I can think of two occasions when we have needed such help. Once I tripped on the edge of a pavement and landed on my face. Another time my wife fell off the path onto the road, and because I was holding her, we both ended in a heap in the middle of the road. People around responded accordingly on both occasions and helped us.

I asked several friends if they would jump forward and help if it occurred in front of them. I received various responses, including, "It depends," with an explanation as to why they might not immediately jump in to help. In fact, it has been proven that the more people there are around, the less likely an individual steps forward to help. There is also a slight reluctance to get involved for fear of liability repercussions. But if you helped, would you do it out of kindness, or would it be a natural reaction because you are human? Would you help a blind person cross the street? I have to believe we would all step forward to help if we saw someone about to put themselves into a life-threatening situation. But would it be out of kindness, or fulfilling a responsibility, or perhaps out of a sense of obligation? Do we, in fact, have an obligation to each other? Are we in any way responsible for each other as fellow human beings?

I remember being in Eastern Europe some years ago and saw a woman sitting on the pavement begging. She had a baby in her arms and I found it a sad and moving sight. It was in the late 1980s and it was the first time I had seen a woman begging. I raised my camera to take a photo, and through the lens it seemed that our eyes met. I could not trigger the shutter. I had an overwhelming sense that I was imposing upon her suffering. The purpose of the photo would have been to share the picture of poverty with people in the West, so that they might provide means to help such people, but did the end justify the means? Perhaps in this instance, it did. Did I miss an opportunity to exercise a moral obligation to share her plight? I am not sure.

DO WE HAVE A MORAL OBLIGATION TO OTHERS?

Looking at the larger picture of poverty and hunger, it is estimated that 800 million people go to bed hungry and another 135 million are on the edge of starvation. I've heard that half the people in the West are obese, while elsewhere millions are undernourished and starving. Is it a distribution problem, an economic problem, or just that governments don't care? Is it that we are unmoved by their plight? Or are we too preoccupied with our own concerns? Are we obligated to help them? Do we carry a responsibility to provide for them? Or is it that occasionally we simply respond emotionally to the suffering because we feel we ought to do something about it? I believe we have a moral obligation to do something, however little it might be.

To fulfill that obligation, we have to love and care for our fellow travelers. We see that Christ did that when on earth. He did not discriminate. He cared for the poor, for the sick, the disfranchised—the less fortunate of this world. He left instructions for his followers to share, to help, to give, to go the extra mile, to be the friend in need, to be a real neighbour to others, and even to do good to enemies. He even said, "Do good to those who spitefully use you." Now that's a tough one. If, however, we have any desire to follow in his footsteps, it would appear that we do have a moral obligation to all people.

Each of us has been given gifts and abilities to fill the role that we play. When we use those gifts to touch the lives of others, we find purpose in our own lives. If we have the experience and the competence to serve others, then we should, in a realistic, sensible, and practical way, offering to play our part in the bigger picture of meeting their needs. We are reminded again that by helping others we help ourselves. There is a law of reciprocity at work in life; namely, that what you give is given back and usually in larger amounts than what you gave. Jesus said that there is nothing greater than being a servant. As we serve others, God can love them through us.

Even if we have a sense of responsibility towards the less fortunate, the starving, the homeless, the poor, the lonely, and the outsiders, how can we fulfill that responsibility when those suffering are half way around the world? When we hear that 90% of the world's children breathe in toxic air every day, millions more drink polluted water, and millions more die from the effects of pollution, we rightly ask, what have we done to this wonderful earth and the atmosphere? If nothing changes we might be the cause of our own extinction. How disturbing it is to see children and adults searching the garbage dumps for a crust of bread, which is the case in India, Africa, and South America! We all know it is impossible for us to reach out and touch all those in need around the world. We cannot be everything to all people. We can, however, reach out to those we can touch, those within our own social circle, the people with whom we mix regularly. We are not called to do everything, but we are called to do something.

I wonder if we take the time to understand fully and appreciate the real circumstances of others around us. Do we really look at people or just give cursory glances? Do we look into their eyes and see what the eyes are saying? To avoid the eyes is to miss the real person inside. Someone once said, "The eyes are the windows of the soul." The eyes say so much. They tell of inward joy or internal struggles. They tacitly share sadness and depression. They can display happiness and expectation. They can speak kindness and gentleness, or anger and aggression. We all speak with our eyes. Learn to listen to the eyes. Observe, instead of just looking. It has been said that to avoid the eyes is to avoid intimacy and a willingness to connect. We must be open to connect if we want to help.

ARE WE IMMUNE TO THE SUFFERING OF OTHERS?

I wonder sometimes if we are too busy with life to be overly concerned about the suffering of others. Do we hear the cries of those hurting? Are we sensitive to their pain or are we able to protect ourselves from it? Do we sympathize or try to empathize, even if we have not been where they are? How many people have committed suicide even after reaching out and sharing their pain, their suffering, and their seeming hopelessness? The American poet Anne Sexton wrote extensively in poems and prose about her struggle with depression. Her book *Live or Die,* for which she received the Pulitzer Prize in 1967, was really a literary cry for help. Her writings reflected an obsession with death and dying. No one recognized or responded to her cry. She committed suicide in 1974 at the age of 44.

Suicide statistics are mind-blowing. Apparently, Europe has the highest rate of suicide. A recent figure showed in excess of 56,000 in one year. It is one of the leading causes of death of men under 45. The average annual suicide rate in the United States is 44,895, which amounts to 123 per day. What is even more disturbing is that attempted suicides are estimated to be 25 times that number. These are not just numbers. They represent people. People who are struggling with the issues of life. People with families who loved them and tried to care for them.

Reports tell us that the highest number of suicides come from people within the health profession, both in North America and Europe. In the United States we are told that a doctor a day commits suicide. This is closely followed by nurses and other medical caregivers. The stress of the occupation and of life causes depression and despair, but it is the stigma of mental illness, particularly from their colleagues, that creates the desire to end it all. I heard of a young 26-year old pediatrician who had a panic attack at work. The next day she committed suicide. Her mother said that she had needed counseling and medication for her depression, but the stigma and fear of losing her job caused her to end her life. It is a tragedy that we as a society don't have a greater understanding of the causes of stress and distress. Perhaps if we did we might be able to offer more care and support, which could save lives.

I read about a gentleman in England who could not deal with the sudden loss of his father. He felt isolated and alone. His grief turned into depression and he wanted to end his life. He sent some final emails to friends, saying he hoped the next few weeks would be good for them. Nobody queried the reasoning behind the messages. He went to the place where he was planning to jump from a bridge or cliff. He put a picture on Facebook to show where he was. People responded with, "A nice place." It seems that deep down he was hoping someone would think his actions strange and come and find him. Finally, a local municipal worker discovered what he was about to do and persuaded him to change his mind. To this day, he is grateful to the man who saw the situation, understood, and reached out to save him from himself. Are we truly listening, or are we too busy living insular and somewhat self-centered lives?

Our world is a sad scenario of suffering, a litany of drug abuse, of addiction, of depression, and mental health issues. Even our friends can become enmeshed in such an unseen battle, to our shock. We have no idea what goes on behind closed doors. We have no concept of what stirs in the minds of others, even friends whom we thought we knew well. We might be amazed at the despair, discouragement, and depressive thoughts with which some people struggle. For some, life is one long battle. Do we not carry some responsibility to care and share, to lift up and support, and encourage where we can? I believe we do.

Few people have not heard the parable of The Good Samaritan. Jesus tells the story of a man on a journey who was set upon by robbers, beaten, and left for dead. Several priests passed that way and walked by on the other side of the road. They had no heart or desire to assist the man. Eventually, a Samaritan came along and reached out to the man, who was a Jew. The Samaritans were enemies of the Jews. Regardless of that, he tended the man's wounds, put him on his donkey, and took him to suitable overnight accommodation. He paid for his stay and promised to reimburse the innkeeper if the costs were more. Jesus asked the question as to who was the real neighbour. It was certainly not the religious leaders of the day who ignored the man. The real neighbour was someone from a group avowed to be enemies. The Samaritan's action came from his heart.

Who is my neighbour? Anyone who comes across my path and is in need. The path today has become very wide. The world is now referred to as a global village, hence no one is very far away. In essence, very few people are out of our reach. Maybe not physically and personally, but through agencies and other people we can touch the lives of millions around the world. We can make a difference. As in the case of the proverbial sand dollar or star fish, we can at least throw one back into the sea and save its life.

SUMMING UP

So do we have some moral obligation to care for each other? I think we do. As Christians, I think even more so. We cannot live in isolation. We are interdependent. We need each other. We are in this life together, and in loving and caring we find friendship, fellowship, and a personal bond as we support and encourage one another. We benefit from the giving. We are lifted to new heights of gratefulness and appreciation when we seek to alleviate the difficulties and suffering of others.

Go out of your way to find a neighbour in need and touch their life. Don't wait until you feel like it. Just do it. Your life will be changed as you seek to change theirs.

CHAPTER 11

Life Is a Spiritual Encounter

In the previous chapters, we have looked at various ways that help us rise above situations that might be pulling us down. We mentioned the benefits of reflection and meditation, the positive results of changing our thinking, and changing our attitudes. We looked at the tough decision of forgiveness and the release it brings. We also saw the extraordinary benefits we receive by reaching out to help others in their plight. All these aspects have therapeutic value, can bring healing, and change our lives for the better.

There is, however, another side to life we often ignore, to our detriment, and that is our spiritual side. We are not just physical bodies with mental capabilities, but spiritual beings. This is confirmed by the innate desire we have to recognize a supreme being. In nations around the world people have historically expressed an inherent need to worship a deity. The seventeenth century philosopher Blaise Pascal suggested that we all have a God-shaped vacuum in our heart, and until that is satisfied we spend our time searching to fill that vacuum, mostly with anything but God. Our spiritual search is really to establish a relationship with God.

From recent religious polls taken, virtually 80% of people in North America say they believe in God—a surprisingly high percentage. If that is true, what do they mean? Do they check that box in the survey rather than list themselves as atheist? I am sure that for some who say they believe, it would be difficult to define the god they believe in. Often he is just a distant being who is acknowledged at special times of the year, such as Easter and Christmas, or at special events like baptisms and funerals. If that is so, then sadly it is a non-personal god who has little to do with the day-to-day issues we face. Yet when we read biographies of people with faith, they indicate that the real God intervenes and is interested in our well-being. Faith is important. Without it one large aspect of our being remains cold and dormant. With it, we gain a spiritual sensitivity and discover a new dimension awakened in us—a spiritual awareness of life.

Maybe you have a faith in God but have never given much thought to the importance of the connection with him, or the fact that God could help you in your everyday situation. I could give you story after story of people who have called out to God at their moment of capitulation, people who have been at the point of suicide, people totally at the end of their rope, nowhere to go, nowhere to turn, and in desperation have asked God to intervene. It is amazing how many people in that situation have started their prayer of help with, "God, if you are there." or "God, if you are real," and have been surprised to find that God was on the other end of the line.

Take Michaela from north-west England, a single mother whose life had become a mess. Escaping from an abusive marriage, she struggled to care for her son. Nothing seemed to go well for her and she succumbed to taking drugs. But it was the unexpected death of a friend that brought her to the breaking point, desperately needing to know what life was really all about. One day in the middle of a panic attack she got on her knees and said, "God, if you are there, do something quick." Immediately, a deep sense of peace came over her, and within a short time God brought people into her life who were able to give counsel and support. She changed from self-hate to understanding how special and valued she was. Her life changed from turmoil to one of serenity and happiness. Michaela discovered that you can never be too low for God to reach down and lift you up and bring restoration.[1]

From what I have read and experienced in life, I believe God is in the business of changing lives. He is interested in us, in fact, in every facet of our lives. There is no aspect of our life that we cannot share with God. There are no problems too difficult or too complicated that he cannot resolve. Our downfall is that we are reluctant to allow him to be involved and intervene in our lives. We want to sort things out ourselves. We feel we can do that. So we struggle along, thinking we know best, and the issues remain unresolved.

Have you ever considered that God might be trying to get your attention? That might sound strange but it could be true. Without being the cause of adverse circumstances, God will certainly use such situations to do just that. I have a friend who was run over by a truck while on his snowmobile. The snowmobile was demolished under the front wheels. My friend should not have lived, but he did. In fact, he never lost consciousness. He maintains that God distinctly talked to him while waiting to be rescued. It totally changed his perspective on life. I also read the story of a businessman who ended up in hospital with a broken back, after having crashed his private plane. He said that it took that event for God to get his attention. Before that he had conveniently ignored God and avoided spiritual matters in his life.

If we allow him, God will intervene in our ordinary, everyday lives and bring solutions to our issues and predicaments. There is no limit to what God can do. He is the God of the miraculous. He heals severed relationships. He brings estranged families together again. He reconciles fathers to sons, mothers to daughters, after years of separation. He can provide food when there is none. He can provide finance when the account is empty. He can bring physical and emotional healing. We have shared stories in this book of courage and determination, where people have overcome serious disadvantages and handicaps, and testify that it was God who gave them the strength.

On a personal basis, my wife and I can attest to experiencing the strength and grace of God in our times of adversity and difficulty. Life is not always easy. In fact, there have been times we faced seemingly insurmountable obstacles. Both my wife and I have had a doctor present us with the cancer diagnosis. On another occasion, we were informed on the telephone late at night that our daughter was being held against her will and was threatened with murder. Those were the times when our faith was really tested. Those were the times when we could do nothing but pray and trust God to intervene. Our faith did not go unrewarded. There have been many other times like those when we were certain of God's intervention.

Perhaps when you hear of God's intervening in the lives of other people, you consider it admirable and encouraging, but then think that your situation is far less dramatic and too mundane for God to be interested and involved. Let me assure you, God is with us in our everyday existence as much as in major traumatic occurrences in life. God is there for us in the never-ending daily routine of home, school, and work. God will meet us right where we are. Right in the middle of our mess. Time and distance are no obstacles to God's performing miracles. I know of an instance in which God resolved a situation in Australia while those concerned were praying in England. We might be limited to time and space, but God is not, and prayer transcends both.

I wonder why are we so reluctant to let God in and allow him to take over? Is it that we think he is too remote? Maybe it is because we think he cannot be interested in small potatoes like us. Perhaps over time God has become distant and impersonal. Maybe it's time to take a closer look. We may be missing out.

Saying we believe in God but not trusting him to change our life or circumstances is like believing that electricity is coming into the house but never switching on the light. Why would we continue to grope around in the dark if we believe we have power coming to the house? Trusting God with our situation is like switching on the light. When we trust God, we move from "I know he can," to "I am going to trust he will." His plans are normally far superior to ours anyway, although we usually think we know better.

The difference between believing and trusting is like this. Imagine the nearest international airport to your home where you know you can get a flight to London. You book your flight, go to the airport and get to the gate. You believe absolutely that the plane will take you to London. However, it is not until you get on the plane, commit yourself to the plane that the plane will take you there. You are now exercising faith and trust in the plane, in the pilot, and in the system that will take you where you want to go, in this case, London. We can say we believe in God, but it is not until we trust him and put our faith in him that we have a personal relationship with him. He remains an absent supreme being somewhere out there. God does not push his way into our lives. He waits to be invited.

I believe it is virtually impossible that one human can convince another human as to the existence of God, but I think God himself is the one who ultimately reveals himself to us when we begin to search for him. We can look at creation and see the hand of intelligent design. We are astounded by the intricacy and harmony of the natural world. We look at the human body and are amazed at its complexity. It is very difficult to believe that this is all the result of a cosmic accident. To me the evidence of a creator is undeniable. Yet it is true that no one has seen God. We cannot describe God physically or visually, but only experience him through his characteristics and his dealings with us as human beings. His characteristics are recorded in the Bible, but they are displayed and demonstrated in his connections with humankind. The obvious direct connection to us was through his son, Jesus Christ, who took on human flesh and lived among us. This is what Christmas is all about. The message of Christmas is one of reconciliation between humanity and God—the building of that relationship.

I am probably on safe ground to say that none of us is perfect. I know I am not. As I have said earlier, we are human and we make mistakes. We have all messed up at some point in our lives. We have done inappropriate things, said inappropriate things, perhaps have had a wrong attitude or been unnecessarily critical, and so on. The extraordinary thing is this. God loves us regardless. His love for us is not contingent upon our actions. We cannot earn his love or his favour. How comforting and reassuring this is, that regardless of how many times we slip or fall or cause disappointment, it does not change the intensity of God's love for us. His love is always there and never decreases or dissipates because of what we do. His love is constant.

There is nothing we need do, or can do, to obtain and benefit from that love. There is no performance, no penance, no good works expected from us to enjoy his love. God knows us and loves us as we are. Once we grasp that concept and accept God's love for us, it will bring an overwhelming sense of being loved, of acceptance, forgiveness, and freedom never before experienced. God gives hope where there is no hope. He brings calmness and peace in the place of turmoil. He can instigate harmony where there is acrimony. He can replace hatred with love. He can change people's hearts, minds, and attitudes. He can do what is beyond our imagination.

God is not concerned about our past mistakes or the present mess we might be in. We don't have to put on a mask or try to be someone whom we are not. We need to be ourselves. God knows us through and through, who we are, what we are, and what we think, yet loves us anyway. God made us, not just physical, but also as spiritual beings, and as such we have this inner desire to experience a relationship with him. We feel lost without it.

Adversity can create the ideal opportunity to begin such a relationship. If you already have faith in God, then adversity can deepen that faith as you allow him to intervene in your life. Things tend not to go away of their own accord. We have to face problems and deal directly with them. The solution may involve other people, their thoughts, their feelings and consideration. It may have to include giving or receiving forgiveness as part of the healing process. God will be involved as we allow him. Once we hand over the situation to him, he will give wisdom to recognize how we go about resolving the issue. We may have to face the music but he will give us strength to do that. He will give us grace to forgive and to understandingly treat others with love and respect.

The result may astound you. Often the people you thought would oppose you and be objectionable will be become uncommonly helpful and assist in finding a solution. God can change the hearts and minds of people even before we request it. I am certain it is not his wish for us to mentally struggle with life, causing us unhappiness, disappointment, and depression. He can provide the strength for us to rise above all adverse circumstances. Whatever mess we are in, he can sort it out. He can bring us to a place of joy and contentment. This is where we move from believing to trusting.

Someone once said, "Adversity introduces a man to himself," which has an element of truth to it, but I think it should read, "Adversity introduces a man to his faith." In our adversity, in the midst of our emotional turmoil, our faith becomes real or it proves non-existent.

SUMMING UP

I once heard someone say that God is a gentleman because he does not force his way into our lives. He invites us to allow him to work out his purpose in us. How do we do that? How do you get God to take over? Ask him, simple as that. Talk to him, but listen as well. Prayer is not just asking God to fix things, it is a conversation. It is a two-way communication. We read in the Bible that if we ask, we will receive. If we seek, we will find. If we knock, the door will be opened. Talk to God. Begin a relationship with him. It is from that relationship that you will receive wisdom, strength, comfort, and peace. It will give you a whole new perspective on life, one you will never regret.

CHAPTER 12

The Real You

"You are exceptional!" What delightful words to hear, especially if they are spoken about you. If we are honest, none of us is immune to a little flattery. To be considered exceptional is uplifting and encouraging. Someone is indicating that you are special even if you might not readily agree. Normally we think we are who we are, and we do what we do. If in doing so others think we are exceptional or special, then that's a bonus. However, I want to tell you that it is the truth; you are exceptional. Perhaps you have never thought about yourself that way but let's consider the word and see how it applies.

We normally equate the word *exceptional* with superior accomplishments, like people who have changed history by their achievements. We are well aware of such names as William Wilberforce, who in the early 1800s worked tirelessly to get slavery abolished. We may think of Albert

Einstein with his brilliant mind and inventive brain. Then more recently we saw Mother Teresa making her impact on the outcasts in Calcutta. These, with many others, accomplished things by which we identify them as being exceptional. Yet there are thousands of regular, unnamed people, people with little public status, solid citizens whose daily effort and dedication to causes and projects makes them outstanding and exceptional. You may be one of those people.

I refer to those people who run or walk or ride for those who are suffering from cancer or other incapacitating diseases. Then there are people who volunteer in shelters for the homeless or the abused. There are those who give up marriage in order to care for a parent. A mother who sacrifices a career to take care of her handicapped child. There are also those who give physical help and get their hands dirty in the support of the less fortunate. These are exceptional people but often unheralded. If you fit into any one of these categories, then you are special and are to be commended.

Most of us however, will not be seen as exceptional in the sphere of changing the world, but that does not diminish our true standing as a valued human being. We willingly acknowledge that, as humans, we have strengths and weaknesses; we have needs, wants, and desires, and we don't always come top of the class. We have learned to accept our humanness with its limitations. However, we need to see ourselves beyond that normality. We need to view ourselves as a person of value, regardless of education, status in society, job, position, and especially regardless of the opinions and views of others. What others think, say, or infer have no bearing, and makes no difference, as to who we are. Each of us is a worthy human being. Nobody can take that away from us.

You are unique. Your uniqueness is invaluable. No one on earth can take your place. You have a purpose for being here. You alone occupy the position you hold and no one else can fill your shoes. You are more than just a face in the crowd. You are more than just a social insurance number. You are important in your own right. You cannot be replaced by another. Value your individuality. Be pleased with who you are. If God made you, then you are special, intrinsically special. God broke the mold when he made you. You are one of a kind. Your worth is beyond question. You are priceless and irreplaceable. There will never be another you. You are significant.

It is not what you do that makes you a valued human being. It is not determined by your occupation. You may be a stay-at-home mom or dad. You may work on an assembly line, wait on tables in a restaurant, you may serve customers in a store. It matters not what you do, it is your inner self that makes you who you are and marks you as being special.

Do you remember the days when you were openly thought special? On the day you were born there was no other child to compare in the eyes of your parents. When you took your first steps, when you first spoke, when you rode your bicycle for the first time—all of these times you were special to those around you. When you appeared in the school drama or represented the school in sports. When you listened to the applause as you received that academic award. When you got your first job and started out in the world of business. You felt special and others around you also acknowledged it. The years may have passed. The dates and events may have changed, but you are still the same person. You are still special to those who love you and care for you. You are very important to those people. They would miss you immensely if you were not around.

Our past has determined where we are at this moment. We have been affected and influenced by people and situations, some good and some not so good. Maybe there are issues that come to mind that have negatively influenced you and need to be dealt with and eradicated. You have carried the hurt with you long enough. You no longer need to be imprisoned by past events or anything detrimental in your past life. You should no longer give the disappointments, failures, and mistakes of yesterday permission to haunt you. This is a new day for you, maybe a new life. You can now move forward to enjoy this new life, being fulfilled and excited. Your life will show that you have reached a new pinnacle in your attitude and acceptance of yourself and who you are. You will recognize that, as a deserving and worthy person, you have a valuable contribution to make to society and others in your social circle. You will begin to demonstrate that you are whole, complete, and have a purpose and reason for living.

Perhaps by now you have already decided it was time for a change in thinking and you've adopted a fresh attitude to life, to yourself, and maybe to others. Maybe you have been thinking it is time you checked things out spiritually and come to understand how that applies to your life. Perhaps you have started a process of forgiveness to clean up some unfinished business. It may take real determination to make a phone call, to send an email, or write a card or note. The effort will be worth it because the rewards are great as you heal a broken relationship. You will find yourself on a new road to peace and joy. This is all part of the result you will experience as you take charge of your situation.

Be strong and determined. Make whatever changes you feel are necessary in order to live your life to the full. You have only one life, so let no one else ruin it for you or try to live it for you. Because of who you are, you have the inner strength to rise above obstacles life might have thrown at you. Go with confidence into the future. The future is yours to claim. Let no one rob you of it. Let no past or present issue dictate your mood and attitude from now on.

When we read what other people have made of their lives, having started with tremendous disadvantages, we find it both inspiring and challenging. I find that so in looking at the life of Christy Brown. He was born in 1932 in Dublin, Ireland, the tenth child in a family of 22 children. He was born with cerebral palsy, which left him completely paralyzed except for some movement in his left foot. Against all odds and enormous difficulties, he learned to write and type with the toes of his left foot. In spite of many hours of intense frustration, often causing him to want to give up, he persevered, and when Christy Brown died in 1981 he was recognized as an accomplished author and painter. His autobiography was entitled, *My Left Foot*. [1]

When we compare our lives to his, it helps us to put things in perspective. I know our lives are far different from his and the issues we have had to deal with are completely unrelated; nonetheless, it is so easy to adopt a "poor me" syndrome caused by the hurts and heartaches we have faced. Yet if we do an honest comparison we have to conclude that we have much for which to be grateful. Christy Brown relied upon other people for his everyday existence, yet he found a reason to work hard and achieve the status of writer and painter. Take a leaf out of his book and stride forward to live the life that God intended for you.

Don't ever lose sight of your worthiness as a human being. As such you are worthy of love. You are worthy to be cared for and to enjoy a life of peace and joy. Never overlook the valuable contribution you have made and are making to the world and those around you. You are important. Never look down on yourself. Stand tall. Walk tall. Be confident. Respect yourself for who you are. Remember, you are your own person. You are unique. You are special. You are exceptional.

Discover your hidden self and enjoy who you really are.

NOTES

CHAPTER 1

1. Jordan B. Peterson, *12 Rules for Life—an antidote to chaos,* Random House Canada, 2018, p.31.

2. Tim Hague, *Perseverance,* Viking Canada, 2018, p.225.

CHAPTER 2

1. Jen Bricker, *Everything Is Possible,* Baker Books, Grand Rapids, Michigan, 2016.

CHAPTER 4

1. Dr. Joe Dispenza, *You Are the Placebo*, Hay House, Inc. USA. 2014.

2. Dr. Caroline Leaf, *Think, Learn, Succeed,* Baker Books, Grand Rapids, Michigan, 2018, p.37

3. Dr. Carol S. Dweck. *Mindset,* Random House, New York, 2006.

4. Sonia Ricotti, *Unsinkable,* New Page Books, Pompton Plains, New Jersey, 2015, p.37.

CHAPTER 5

1. Robert Greene. *The Laws of Human Nature*, Profile Books, London, 2018.

2. Viktor E. Frankl. *Man's Search for Meaning*, Rider, London, 2004, p.148.

CHAPTER 6

1. The story of Chris Williams accident can be read at www.elitereaders.com

2. Dr. S.L. McMillen, *None of these Diseases*, Fleming H Revell Company, Westwood, New Jersey, 1963.

3. The stories of Jake and Sarah were discovered in general research.

4. The well-known story of Amy Biehl can be found in many places, one of which is in the May 3rd 2016 edition of the *Orange County Register* at www.ocregister.com.

CHAPTER 7

1. Robert S. McGee, *The Search for Significance*, Thomas Nelson, Dallas, Texas, 2003, p.11

CHAPTER 9

1. Nick Vujicic, *Life without Limits*, Waterbrook, New York, 2018.

2. Bob Harrison, son of Edna Harrison Harlin, *PowerPoints for Success*, Whitaker House, New Kensington, PA, 2004, p.92.

3. Erik Rees, *Never Ever Give Up*, Zondervan, Grand Rapids, Michigan. 2014.

CHAPTER 11

1. The story of Michaela is from *The God Who Changes Lives,* Editor, Mark Elsdon-Dew, HTB Publications, London. 1998, p.25.

CHAPTER 12

1. Christy Brown, *My Left Foot*, Vintage, 1991.

A word from the author...

I hope you have enjoyed reading the book. If you know someone who might be encouraged by reading it, perhaps you could share your copy or suggest they obtain their own. And one last thing. Would you take a few moments now, go to the Amazon page where the book is, and leave a line or two of review. This is important for others and very helpful to me. I would be most appreciative. Thanks

John Murray.

To connect with the author:
email: murray150@fastmail.fm
twitter: @AuthorJMurray
facebook.com/AuthorJohnMurray
website: http://www.jmurray.ca

To order more copies of this book, find books by other Canadian authors, or make inquiries about publishing your own book, contact PageMaster at:

PageMaster Publication Services Inc.
11340-120 Street, Edmonton, AB T5G 0W5
books@pagemaster.ca
780-425-9303

catalogue and e-commerce store
PageMasterPublishing.ca/Shop

About the Author

John has been married to his wife Rita for almost 60 years. They have two children, five grandchildren and two great-grandchildren. Originally from the U.K. they now reside in White Rock, British Columbia, on the west coast of Canada.

Educated in England, John went on to study theology in Birmingham, U.K. and in Toronto, Canada. His life experience has been in business, in journalism, in pastoral ministry and overseas missions.

For the last twenty years before retiring he served as the Executive Director for Eurovangelism Canada, a mission working in Eastern Europe. He travelled extensively from Russia in the north to Albania in the south. Some of the stories in the book *Miracles: Coincidence or Divine Intervention* are from his days travelling in Eastern Europe.

His many years of speaking engagements took him to ten countries which included Canada, the United States, the United Kingdom, Europe and the Caribbean.

Since retiring in 2006 he has concentrated on his writing. *Discover Your Hidden Self* is his fourth book.